If These Walls Could Talk

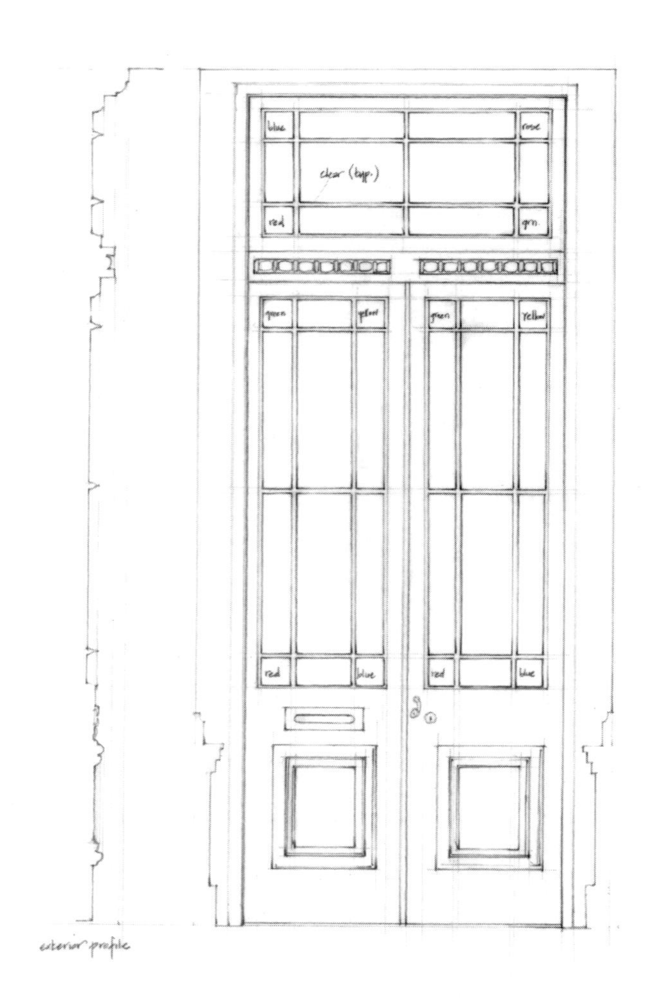
blue
rose
clear (typ.)
red
grn.
green
yellow
green
yellow
red
blue
red
blue
exterior profile

IF THESE WALLS COULD TALK

Victoria's Houses from the Past

By

Valerie Green

Illustrated by Lynn Gordon-Findlay

TouchWood Editions

First edition

TouchWood Editions are an imprint of Horsdal & Schubart Publishers Ltd., Victoria, BC, Canada.

Cover and book design by Public Art & Design, Victoria, BC.
Cover illustrations by Lynn Gordon-Findlay, Victoria, BC.

We acknowledge the support of The Canada Council of the Arts for our publishing program. We also wish to acknowledge the financial support of the Government of Canada through the Book Publishing Industry Development Program (BPDIP) for our publishing activities. We also acknowledge the financial support of the Province of British Columbia through the British Columbia Arts Council.

This book is set in Bodoni.
Printed and bound in Canada by Friesens, Altona, Manitoba.

National Library of Canada Cataloguing in Publication Data

Green, Valerie, 1940-
If these walls could talk

Includes bibliographical references and index.
ISBN 0-920663-78-8

1. Historic buildings–British Columbia–Victoria. 2. Dwellings–British Columbia–Victoria–History. 3. Victoria (B.C.)–History. 4. Victoria (B.C.)–Biography. I. Gordon-Findlay, Lynn, 1960- II. Title.
FC3846.7.G73 2001 971.1'28 C2001-911173-8
F1089.5.V6G73 2001

Printed and bound in Canada

Contents

Dedications

This book is for my parents (my past)
David (my present)
and Matthew and Kate (my future)
and is dedicated to all those who recognize the value of our heritage.

Valerie Green

For my two treasures, Cameron Mark and Ross Alexander.

Lynn Gordon-Findlay

Acknowledgments

During the course of researching and writing the histories of these Greater Victoria homes, I was both amazed and delighted to discover the pride displayed by the current owners in the heritage of each house. This would be understandable if the houses had been in their families for generations, but I found the same enthusiasm from residents who had only recently taken over ownership, and had no connection with past owners. All were fascinated to learn what had happened there in days gone by, and all were anxious to share more stories with me.

I would, therefore, like to thank all the owners for taking the time to talk with me about their homes and/or inviting me to visit. My particular thanks go to Clare and Dennis Atkinson, Mel Bolen, Bob Carmichael, Terese (Todd) Cateriano, Sheila Colwill, Bayne Dean, Mrs. P.E. Ellis, Sandra Gray, Howard Griffin, Ruth Holmes, Gerri and Rob Laundy, Pat Martin Bates, Marilyn Norman, Sherri Robinson, Brad and Tracy Shuya, Jean Sparks, Valerie Terry, Derek Todd and Jean Vantreight, for their interest and their inspiration.

In addition, my thanks to the British Columbia Archives, the Royal B.C. Museum, the Hudson's Bay Company Archives, the Victoria, Esquimalt, Saanich, Oak Bay and Saanich Pioneers' Society archives, and the Victoria Art Gallery, for their staffs' co-operation and assistance. Special thanks also to Peter Salmon, editor of *The Islander* magazine, for his initial interest in a "Houses from the Past" series, and to Pat Touchie and Marlyn Horsdal for their enthusiasm for and faith in this project.

Without the help of all of the above, and without the added bonus of Lynn Gordon-Findlay's exceptional artwork, this book would not have come to fruition.

Valerie Green

Maps

Downtown Area

1. 2616 Pleasant Street
2. 998 Humboldt Street
3. 146 Clarence Street
4. 721 Linden Street
5. 1423 Fernwood Road
6. 601 Trutch Street

Rockland Area

7. 1462 Rockland Avenue
8. 1021 Gillespie Place
9. 638 Rockland Place
10. 1041 St. Charles Street

Esquimalt

11. 507 Head Street
12. 820 Dunsmuir Road and 1024 Munro Street
13. 639 Admirals Road
14. 1211 Old Esquimalt Road
15. 1165 Old Esquimalt Road
16. 1010 Arcadia Street
17. 572 Head Street

Gorge Area

18. 516 Gorge Road West
19. 2895 Colquitz Avenue

Saanich Area

20. Dodd House
21. 4423 Tyndall Avenue
22. 4320 Torquay Drive
23. 1861 Ferndale Road
24. 1775 Barrie Road
25. 1542 Mt. Douglas X Road
26. 1279 Tattersall Drive
27. 1140 Tattersall Drive
28. 3301 Camrose Court
29. 1911 Woodley Road
30. 4366 Blenkinsop Road

Pleasant St.
Bay Street
Blanshard Street
Fernwood Rd.
Begbie St.
Pandora Street
Fort Street
Johnson St.
St. Charles St.
Joan Cres.
Trutch St.
Gillespie Pl.
Richardson St.
Humboldt St.
Fairfield Rd.
Rockland Pl.
Linden Ave.
Clarence St.
Simcoe St.
Vancouver St.
Niagara St.
Downtown and Rockland Area

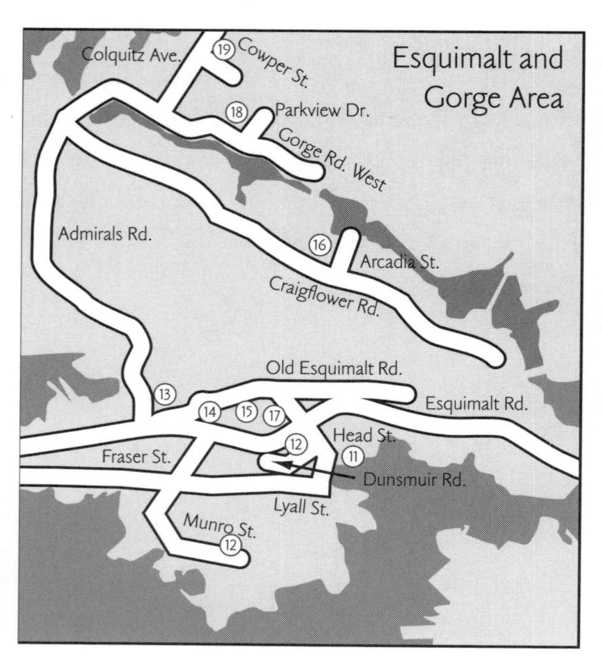

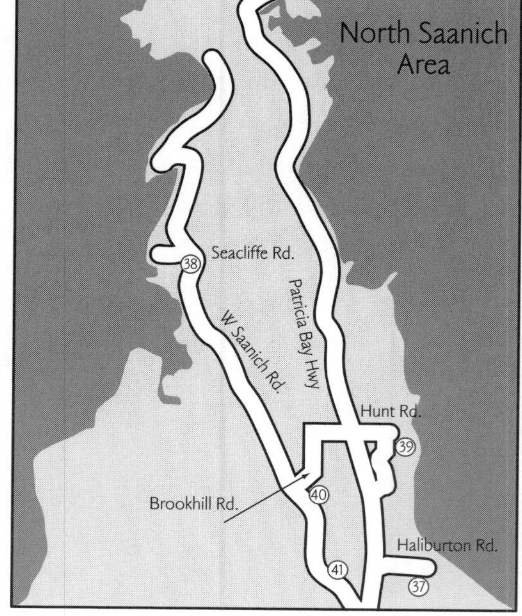

31. 4201 Quadra Street
32. 762 Ralph Street
33. 3808 Heritage Lane
34. 588 Ridgegrove Avenue
35. 931 Woodhall Drive
36. 1248 Burnside Road West
37. 975 Haliburton Road
38. 600 Seacliffe Road
39. 6187 Hunt Road
40. 5789 Brookhill Road
41. 4794 West Saanich Road

Oak Bay

42. 2564 Heron Street
43. 1932 St. Ann Street
44. 2031 Runnymede Avenue
45. 2391 Beach Drive
46. 1587/1595 York Place
47. 356 Newport Avenue
48. 3150 Rutland Road
49. 2087 Byron Street
50. 1255 Victoria Avenue

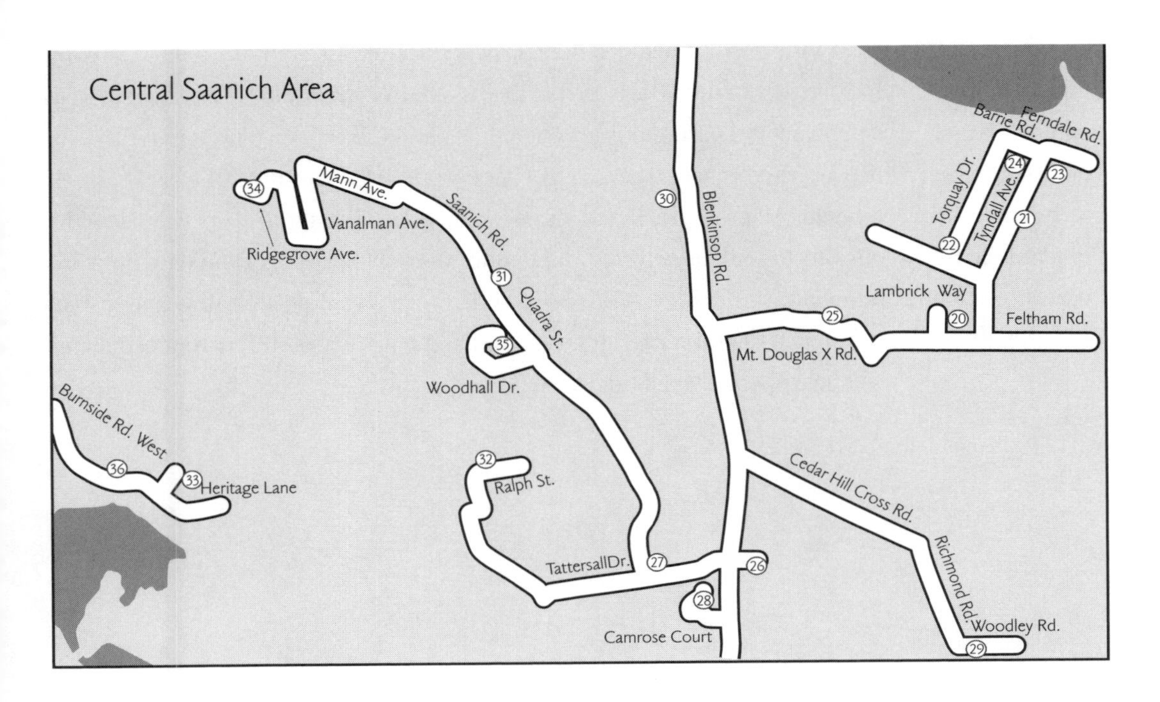

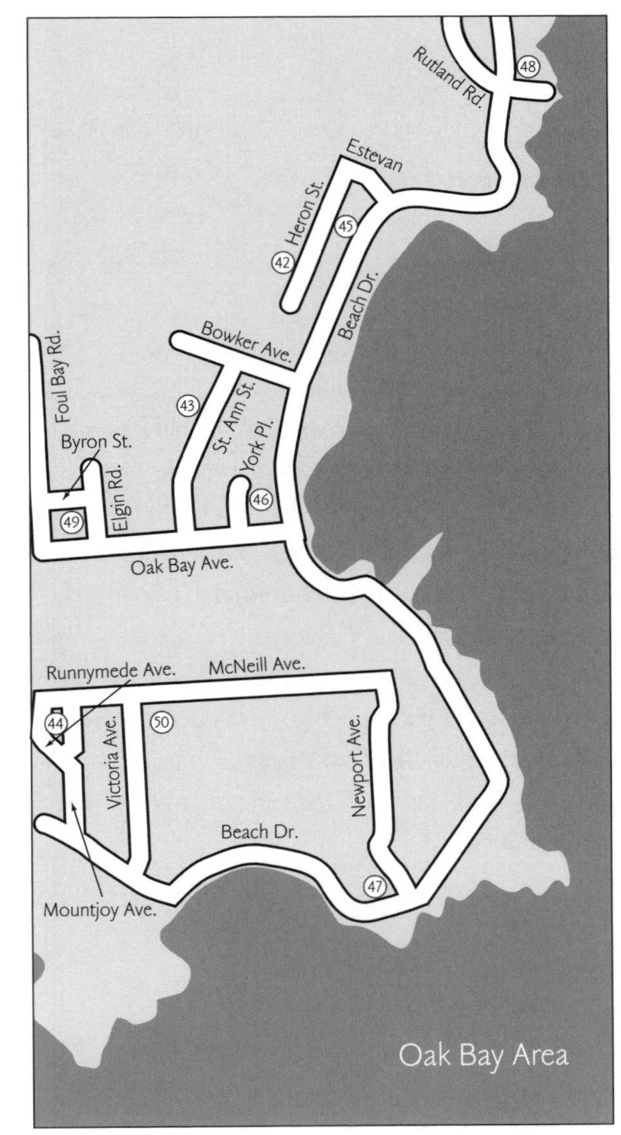

Introduction

Throughout time, a house has been considered something of a status symbol. This was especially true in early Victoria where the more elegant the domicile, the more wealthy and well-established were its inhabitants. In those days, to be a person of importance invariably meant to be a "person of property."

Today, the status quo has changed and we tend to judge people less by the houses in which they live. Nonetheless, many people still have an innate curiosity about the interiors of other people's houses. A house and its trimmings tell us much about its current and past owners. I found this particularly true as I began my journey through the archival histories of many of Greater Victoria's houses, and I especially enjoyed hearing stories of the events that had taken place in those houses through the years: the more bizarre and unusual stories playing a big part in deciding which houses to include here. The idea for this book was originally based on a successful series entitled "Houses from the Past" which ran in *The Islander* section of the *Times Colonist* in 2000.

Lynn Gordon-Findlay's drawings of these homes are all architectural masterpieces. However, the text does not concentrate specifically on the structure or style of the buildings as much as the interesting anecdotes that came to light in their histories. The result is an interesting mix of elegant houses, coupled with ordinary homes – in all shapes, sizes and designs – their common factor being an unusual, ofttimes quirky, story from their past.

All the houses included here, except one, are still standing today. Ranging in origin from the 1850s to the 1930s, all, to a greater or lesser degree, can be considered part of our heritage. Each house has been placed in its respective area and is accompanied by background information on the area's development. Maps are included showing the house locations. This will allow the curious to walk or drive by and ponder those happenings from days gone by. Some are still private residences while others are now multi-dwelling establishments. In either case, it is hoped that the privacy of the current occupants will be respected at all times.

Downtown Area

Victoria began as a fort in 1843, became a gold-rush tent-town in 1858, and eventually earned city status in 1862.

During those turbulent first years and through all the decades since, the City of Victoria has seen numerous changes in the buildings that have housed her residents. Houses for the first settlers were all built of wood.

Governor James Douglas, with the assistance of Joseph Pemberton, the colonial surveyor, compiled a town plan for the city. Its boundaries were initially somewhat limited and it would be many years before a "Greater Victoria" took shape, encompassing James Bay, Fernwood, Rockland, Esquimalt, Oak Bay and Saanich.

Three of the more famous residences from early times still exist – Point Ellice House, Carr House and Helmcken House – and all are currently open to the public, allowing the curious to step back in time.

One of these, Point Ellice House, has been included in this text, along with five other lesser-known homes within the city limits, dating from the 1860s to the 1920s. Their stories include love affairs which came to nothing, reputed ghosts, a special wedding gift, a little aviation history, a family den with a connection to the Blaine Peace Arch, some amateur theatricals and social events in the home of British Columbia's first lieutenant-governor.

A veritable mix of city tales!

POINT ELLICE HOUSE

AN OASIS OF ROMANCE, INTRIGUE AND MYSTERY

Situated as it is in the midst of Victoria's industrial land, "Point Ellice House" at 2616 Pleasant Street still manages to hold its own almost 140 years after it was built along the banks of the Gorge Arm. A veritable oasis of tranquil beauty, it retains the mystique of the Victorian era while surrounded by the commercial noise and hubbub of the twenty-first century.

The original building was described as "a cottage overlooking the Gorge waterway" and was designed by John Wright in 1861 for Charles W. Wallace, a steamboat and mining man. It is one of the oldest existing houses in Victoria. Point Ellice House, however, with its many alterations and additions designed by John Teague and W.R. Wilson through the years, has always been considered the O'Reilly family home.

Peter O'Reilly, the colony's first gold commissioner, had married Caroline Trutch in 1863 in a picturesque December wedding held at Christ Church Cathedral and, after a short sojourn in New Westminster where the first of their four children was born, the couple returned to Victoria. O'Reilly then purchased the attractive Gorge waterway cottage from Wallace for the sum of $2,500 and he and his wife raised three more children there.

As his family increased and his position in society improved, O'Reilly carried out significant additions to the house. There were twelve rooms and seven fireplaces and a kitchen with a built-in French range and brick inside chimney. Much of the original interior decor still exists today, including the wallpaper, the O'Reilly furniture, and some Persian rugs.

The grounds were also improved through the years with several outbuildings added – stables, a carriage house, a greenhouse and a boathouse. Point Ellice House also boasted one of the finest lawn tennis courts and croquet lawns in Victoria and was in fact the site of the first lawn tennis tournament in Victoria. Being at the centre of social activity among the elite, the O'Reillys played host to numerous skating parties, summer picnics, riding, and boating activities at their property. The yearly Gorge regattas in May always meant open house at Point Ellice with visits from naval personnel and other influential members of high society, including one dinner party at which Prime Minister John A. Macdonald and his wife were the guests of honour.

Kathleen O'Reilly, the O'Reillys' only surviving daughter, was born at Point Ellice in 1867, a few short weeks after the family had moved in, and spent all her life there, eventually dying in 1945 in the home she loved. Despite her great beauty, many suitors, and at least one documented proposal of marriage, Kathleen never wanted to leave Point Ellice to marry, and has therefore remained a source of fascination for historians who were intrigued by her many love affairs. Her numerous beaux included such notables as Captain Stanhope (heir to an earldom) and Robert Scott (of South Pole fame), but all her romances came to nothing.

There is another side to the story of Point Ellice House and this touches on the paranormal. Through the years there have been a number of ghost sightings on or near the site. Experts on this subject claim there are possibly four reasons to explain these apparitions. First, the fact that one prominent family inhabited Point Ellice for over 100 years would make for a strong presence felt in the house and its grounds. Secondly, the house is close to water which conducts the "energy" necessary for ghostly appearances. In addition, the house, once peacefully situated, is now in the midst of the noise and turmoil of an industrial area. And lastly, the collapse of the Point Ellice Bridge in 1896, killing over fifty people, happened in close proximity to the house. Any disaster such as this is likely to produce an aftermath of electric emotion. Whether or not these elements contribute to the appearance of ghosts at Point Ellice is debatable, but many people claim that sightings have indeed occurred.

Point Ellice ghosts are included in an account by two Australian women tourists during the 1960s who had camped on the grounds near the water. Point Ellice House was uninhabited at that time. Sometime during the night, the women awoke to a female's disapproving voice ordering them off the property. They immediately began to gather up their things, only to discover that there was nobody there. Continuing to feel waves of hostility surrounding them, they eventually departed. Family members believed the voice was that of Caroline O'Reilly.

Caroline's son, Frank, who died in 1941, has also been heard in the hallway near his room in Point Ellice House in the 1980s, and in 1995, while filming at the house during the Commonwealth Games in Victoria, the Canadian Broadcasting Corporation was reported to have "captured" a ghost on their news footage.

An even stranger story concerns a group of tourists in the 1970s who arrived at the house one day wanting a tour. John O'Reilly and his wife, Inez, ran the house as a museum at that time. Inez had been working in the garden so she asked the tourists to wait while she tidied up and then would give them a tour. Upon her return, they told her to thank the "lady in the blue costume period dress" who had escorted them through the house. Inez was puzzled and took them to Kathleen O'Reilly's room to show them a blue dress which had belonged to Kathleen and was always laid out on her bed. The tourists agreed that the "lady" who escorted them was indeed wearing that dress. Had Kathleen returned some thirty years after her death to give one last tour?

Many people also claim that a light is sometimes seen at night passing back and forth underneath the Point Ellice Bridge. It has no apparent source, but many believe it is the ghost of someone searching for a loved one lost in the tragedy of 1896.

Truth or fiction? Whatever the real explanation for these occurrences, one thing is abundantly clear. Walking through Point Ellice House today or strolling through the beautiful surrounding gardens, it is very easy to take a step back in time and imagine Kathleen, her parents, or other members of the family walking that same route. Their presence is still very apparent decades after their deaths.

In the 1960s members of the family opened the house as a private museum, but since December 1974, the house has been owned by the provincial government which now runs it as a heritage attraction.

2616 Pleasant Street

THE BEACONSFIELD

A WEDDING GIFT FOR A BELOVED DAUGHTER

In 1904 when Gertrude Rithet married Lawrence Genge, the bride's father, Robert Rithet, presented his daughter with a most extravagant wedding present.

No simple gift of furniture or silverware would have been good enough for this bride, for being her father's only daughter, she was loved beyond measure. Robert was a wealthy, well-established merchant in Victoria and could easily afford to bestow upon his daughter a splendid home of her own on Humboldt Street, not far from his own estate, "Hollybank." The address of the house Robert Rithet built for his daughter and new son-in-law was 998 Humboldt and, although it has been slightly modified through the years, the Genge house still stands there today.

The giving of houses as wedding presents had become something of a tradition in the Rithet family, because when Robert had married Elizabeth Munro in 1875, her father, Alexander Munro, a retired Hudson's Bay Company factor, had given them Hollybank as a wedding gift. It was there that their three children (including Gertrude) were born and raised.

Hollybank stood at 952 Humboldt Street and in its day was one of Victoria's finest homes. It was situated on a large slice of land to the east of the old St. Joseph's Hospital and was surrounded by a beautiful iron fence and numerous holly trees from which it took its name. Shortly after Elizabeth Rithet's death in 1952, Hollybank was demolished, but a piece of the railing was saved and removed to the grounds of the provincial museum. Today, that railing surrounds James Douglas' cherry tree which he had planted there in 1854.

When Gertrude announced to her parents that she intended to marry Lawrence A. Genge, whose family lived nearby at Humboldt and Vancouver, they deemed it right and proper that their daughter should have a home just as splendid as the one in which she had grown up. Building it near their own property meant that Gertrude and her mother would still be able to ride there or across the open countryside together, a pastime the two women particularly enjoyed.

The Rithet/Genge wedding was a splendid affair, a memorable event in early Victoria. Gertrude's dress was of white crepe de chine trimmed with duchess lace and she carried a bouquet of roses. Her wedding set a precedent because she had chosen her bridesmaids' dresses to be of Nile green complete with white chiffon fichus (triangular-shaped shawls) and picturesque poke bonnets. The fact that the bridesmaids' dresses were coloured rather than the traditional whites and creams had broken the rules of society. Previously a coloured dress was thought to have been too bold a contrast in an ensemble where the primary purpose was to enhance the bride, not her attendants. Gertrude, however, was a striking woman of beauty who would most probably have stood out in any gathering.

998 Humboldt Street

The following year, 998 Humboldt Street was ready for the newlyweds to move in, and for many years thereafter Mrs. Rithet and Mrs. Genge enjoyed one another's company over tea, or out exercising their horses as they headed for Beacon Hill Park or the surrounding countryside.

The Genge home was designed by Samuel Maclure, the top architect of the day. Originally its appearance was described as a "rather disorganized facade consisting of a veranda extension on one side, balanced by an integral entrance porch on the other."

In 1913, however, Maclure was re-hired by the Genges to add a sunroom gallery across the front of the house which would unify the elevation at the ground-floor level. The entrance door was then placed between two free-standing columns. This effect was re-enforced by adding a central roof dormer. The style of the Genges' home now became formal beaux-arts classical as opposed to the previous arts and crafts style.

Gertrude and her two brothers both died before their mother, Elizabeth, who lived until 1952, one year short of her 100th birthday. Gertrude Genge had passed away in 1945, and her brothers, John and Edward, some years earlier, so fortunately none of them lived to witness the demise of Hollybank, the house they had all grown up in and loved.

The Rithet business operations of real estate, export/import and insurance were carried on through Rithet's son-in-law, Lawrence, and later his grandson, J.R. Genge, after Robert's death in 1919. But Victoria still remembers the name of Rithet in numerous ways. The building at 1117 Wharf Street which had once housed the offices of R.P. Rithet & Company Limited, was a familiar Victoria landmark. Rithet Street in James Bay and Rithetwood in Broadmead are both named for Robert Rithet whose 700-acre Broadmead property, where he once bred champion horses, is now an upper middle-class subdivision of fine homes. And Rithet's Bog in Saanich also perpetuates the Rithet name.

Equally important and often overlooked, is the house he gave his beloved daughter as a wedding gift at the turn of the twentieth century. It still stands on Humboldt Street and is today better known as the Beaconsfield Bed & Breakfast. Through the years it has been restored in a turn-of-the-century mode with particular attention to various aspects of Gertrude and Lawrence Genge's life in the home they once cherished.

Guest rooms at the Beaconsfield are charmingly decorated in Victorian and Edwardian style, and today honeymoon couples frequently spend time there, enjoying the romantic ambience from the past.

146 CLARENCE STREET

THE BIRD MAN'S HOUSE

What is the connection between a field on the old Dean Heights farm (near present-day Lansdowne School), and a house on Clarence Street in James Bay?

The house in question is 146 Clarence Street, built around 1885 for a family called Goepels. The link between it and that once-bumpy field in Saanich concerns an incredible man named William Wallace Gibson who was a later owner of the Clarence Street house and who made aviation history in that field ninety years ago.

Clarence Street itself is named for the Goepels' son, Clarence. Their house was typical of the many rather ordinary, Italianate, two-storey houses built at that time, with some alterations and additions made through the years. What makes this house historically important and far from ordinary, however, is that when Gibson owned it some rather extraordinary things occurred there.

Gibson was born in Ayrshire, Scotland, in 1874, and emigrated to Canada (Saskatchewan) as a young man. From his days of flying kites as a youngster, he had been intrigued by the possibility of man taking to the air and flying. In 1904 he made a model airplane using the roller from a window blind to propel it. He was so encouraged by his initial success that he went on to work on other designs. At that time, however, anyone interested in the possibility of man one day flying was thought to be somewhat strange, so Gibson remained secretive about his accomplishments.

Following some success in a gold-mining expedition, Gibson headed for Vancouver Island in 1907 and purchased the Clarence Street house. For a while he worked in real estate, but soon returned to his hobby and began making a number of large-scale model planes which he tested out in nearby Beacon Hill Park. He then chose the model which gave the best performance and designed a plan from it for a full-sized, four-cylinder, two-cycle, fifty-horsepower engine and airframe machine.

With the $10,000 he had received from a gold claim on the Elk River, he was able to pay the Hutchison Brothers machine shop in Victoria to complete the engine, which weighed in at 210 pounds and drove two contra-rotating propellers. He assembled the rest of his airplane himself in the coach house which once stood at the rear of 146 Clarence Street.

The twenty-foot wings were covered with blue silk supplied by Fred Jeune of Jeune Brothers on Johnson Street, and Tom Plimley of automobile fame provided the undercarriage consisting of four bicycle wheels. The pilot's seat was simply a western saddle strapped in front of the engine. In Gibson's own words: "With spruce and cedar, silk and wire, /Our bird began to show attire." He named his creation *Twin Plane.*

Once the masterpiece was successfully assembled, Gibson took it completely apart again in order to transport the pieces in a horse-drawn wagon to its launching site, the field on the Lansdowne slope, south of Mount Tolmie.

And there, on that momentous morning of September 8, 1910, Gibson carried out his maiden flight. The plane barely lifted off the ground, flying only for approximately 200 feet before landing heavily and smashing one of its wheels – but it was a beginning.

Two weeks later, with wheel now repaired, Gibson mounted his saddle seat yet again and attempted a second, more successful, flight. This time he even landed the plane in one piece, despite heading straight into an oak tree and sustaining some minor injuries himself. Nonetheless, that September, aviation history had been made by William Wallace Gibson.

Gibson continued to make more improvements to his design and eventually undertook demonstration flights at Kamloops and Calgary with a newly built six-cylinder engine. He was finally persuaded by his concerned wife, who by then had witnessed far too many costly crashes, that he should stop flying and move to California. He reluctantly agreed and then went on to become a most successful businessman.

Gibson also wrote a book entitled *The Bird Man* and was made an honorary Cree Indian chief with a name that translated as "Chief Flash in the Sky Boy." He died in California in November 1965 at the age of ninety-one.

Gibson's second engine still exists at the National Aviation Museum in Ottawa; a reproduction of *Twin Plane* was constructed in 1987 by the British Columbia Aviation Museum under the provincial Job Trac program, and is on display at the Sidney museum at the Victoria Airport on Vancouver Island.

In 1928, Lansdowne Field, the site of Gibson's first attempt at aviation glory, was officially opened as British Columbia's first licensed airport, after having been purchased the year before by B.C. Airways.

Years after his incredible maiden flight in Victoria, Gibson reminisced about his experiences on that day. He said: "Imagine a man teetering on the edge of the first skyscraper, praying he won't plunge to his death. Then you'll have an idea how I felt on that September morning...."

And Gibson House on Clarence Street, which is now a multi-dwelling residence, remains as a monument to this pioneer. It is still acknowledged as being the site where pioneer aviator, William Wallace Gibson, constructed western Canada's first aircraft.

146 Clarence Street

BLYTHEHOLM

THE HOUSE WHERE PEACE REIGNED SUPREME

Today it is a fairly ordinary-looking, multi-dwelling house on a tree-lined street in Victoria, but a few decades ago 721 Linden Avenue was a hub of activity. More importantly, one room in this home, namely the den, was where numerous important decisions of the day were made.

Many houses in the 700 and 800 block of Linden were constructed between 1905 and 1913. Number 721, the home of newlyweds Bert Todd and his bride, the former Ada Seabrook, was one of them. The Todds had made history after their Los Angeles wedding in March of 1910 with a honeymoon trip north by automobile to Vancouver Island. This was to become a pathfinding journey of great significance. In fact, the Todds' automobile trek was the forerunner of all Pacific coastal travel and the inspiration behind a permanent Pacific highway. Upon their arrival in Victoria, Bert and Ada Todd soon settled into their new home on Linden Avenue and named it "Blytheholm."

Originally the main floor of the house consisted of a front porch area, a vestibule, a living room, a den, a dining room, a butler's pantry, and a very large kitchen and half bathroom. A stairway off the living room led to the master bedroom with fireplace and bathroom, a sleeping porch, two more bedrooms and another full bathroom. There was also a back staircase off the kitchen leading to the domestics' quarters and a laundry room.

The house also contained something that few during that period would have had: a garage built in the basement. The presence of this added feature, however, was hardly surprising because Bert Todd, son of salmon-canning magnate, Jacob Hunter Todd, and a future mayor of Victoria, was a car fanatic and dedicated his entire life to pioneering for better highway systems throughout the Pacific Northwest.

His passion for the automobile had begun in the spring of 1903 when he set off in his newly purchased "White Steam" along the Gorge Road heading towards Sooke. The journey had been made without benefit of insurance, driver's licence, licence plates, registration, windshield, or fenders (none of which were necessary by the standards of the day). Todd's vision for the future of the automobile would also ultimately encourage the increase of tourism to the area.

In those early years of residence on Linden Avenue, Bert and Ada Todd were also raising their two sons: Joe, born in 1911, and Dick, in 1913. The couple loved to entertain and many well-known Victoria citizens spent time at their home. Bert's favourite expression as he greeted his guests was "Come in and let's inspect the boiler" which simply meant "Let's have a Scotch and soda."

Bert also enjoyed pottering at his workbench in the basement or in his large garden. The garden was divided by a fence running north to south, the east end being a vegetable garden while the west end was grass and flowers with a "garden house" in the southwest corner. The vegetable garden covered about 3,000 square feet and enabled the Todds to produce a considerable

721 Linden Avenue

amount of vegetables both for themselves and for sale to James Adams, "The Particular Grocer," in the Fort Building. There were also dog kennels and a chicken coop with about thirty Rhode Island Reds producing fresh eggs. The Todds were so passionate about their gardening and, in particular, their "pea patch," that Ada did not object when one year one of her birthday gifts from Bert was a load of manure!

Her October engagement present back in 1909 had been somewhat more exciting, however. Bert had given her the "October Mansion," an apartment building no less, which still stands today at the corner of Fort and Cook streets.

It was Bert's den, however, that held many fascinating secrets while the Todds were in residence. It was in that room, while he was first alderman and then mayor, that Todd had entertained many of his colleagues and made decisions concerning the running of the city. Also in the den, with his American friend, millionaire Sam Hill (whose name it was said had inspired the expression "what in the name of Sam H..l!"), discussions had been held concerning the possibility of raising money for a peace monument to be erected at the border between Canada and the United States. The men decided that donations should be made by the children of both countries and among the first to donate were Bert's two young sons, Joe and Dick. The names of all the donating children were then written on a scroll which, together with other memorabilia, was placed in a time capsule inside the monument at the dedication ceremony in 1921. Although those initial donations raised several thousand dollars, it was Sam Hill who paid most of the reported $260,000 for the building of the Peace Arch at Blaine which still stands today as a symbol of peace between the two countries: an idea which had germinated in a den on Linden Avenue in Victoria.

On August 10, 1927, Bert Todd rose early and went to work in his den as was his usual custom when suddenly he collapsed and fell to the floor. It took many months for his doctors to fully diagnose Bert's problem, a brain tumour. He was admitted to a hospital in Seattle for brain surgery in October of 1928, but did not survive the operation. His death caused an outpouring of sorrow throughout the city of Victoria.

According to later city directories, Blytheholm lay vacant in 1929. In 1931, the residence was owned by one R.R. Sutherland, but by the 1950s, the large house had been converted into apartments. In the mid-1970s, it was known as the "Glendower Apartments."

Today, 721 Linden is still a multi-dwelling residence but remains an intriguing house holding many secrets from the past within its walls.

1423 FERNWOOD ROAD

THE J.L. BECKWITH FAMILY HOME

At one time, both Jean (Beckwith) Vantreight's maternal and paternal grandparents lived on Fernwood Road in Victoria: her mother's parents lived at 1919 Fernwood (near the Belfry Theatre) and her Beckwith grandparents at 1423 Fernwood. This story concerns the Beckwiths' family home.

Grandfather, John Leander Beckwith, was born in Cornwallis, King's County, Nova Scotia, in 1857, and came to Victoria in 1884 via Portland, Oregon. His arrival in Victoria coincided with that of Charles W. Rogers, later of chocolate fame. The two men became acquainted, and when Rogers seemed despondent about the course of his life, Beckwith advised and encouraged him to pursue his dream, which had always been to make exceptional candy. Beckwith even procured a marble slab from a local mortuary on which Rogers could roll out his candy.

Describing himself as a "commercial traveller," Beckwith had already worked in the retail clothing and dry goods businesses. From 1885 until 1890, he represented H. Sherry & Co. of Montreal, and later operated a general commission outfit as agent for Mannbyars & Co. of Glasgow. Then in 1905, he started his own company in Victoria, J.L. Beckwith & Co., and was the broker for the Clayoquot Sound Canning Company which canned fish on Vancouver Island's west coast.

Always affectionately known as "J.L.," he easily earned the reputation of "a very public-spirited gentleman." He was always very concerned with trying to better the community around him. He and his wife, Agnes McLeod of Berwick, Nova Scotia, raised three children (Harold, Fred and Grace) in their Fernwood home which was built in the early 1890s. The Beckwiths were very interested in education and deemed it most important for the future well-being of their children and others in the area.

J.L. therefore made it his business to promote secondary education in Victoria which, by the turn of the century, he felt was sadly lacking. He was largely responsible for the establishment in 1903 of Victoria College which was originally affiliated with McGill University. Then, when the University of British Columbia opened in 1915, Victoria College ceased to operate, but with Beckwith's input and perseverance it eventually re-opened in 1920 at Craigdarroch Castle. All three Beckwith children graduated from McGill – Harold in arts, Fred in medicine, and Grace in geology, so J.L.'s passionate belief in higher education certainly paid off in his own family.

A moral and religious way of life was paramount in the Beckwiths' Fernwood home. Mealtimes always began with grace followed by a time for sharing the day's experiences. The children were then given the opportunity to express their thoughts and feelings on many subjects as they sat around the table.

In addition, because of the family's great interest in theatre, amateur theatrical productions were encouraged in the home. The design of the house certainly lent itself to amateur performances. Cedar panelling lined the walls of the living and dining rooms which were separated by an archway. When hung with curtains, this served as a perfect opening to a makeshift stage. Shakespeare's works were always popular with the family, especially *Macbeth*, and the children delighted in showing off their talents to friends at these performances.

J.L.'s involvement with the issues of the day included many things. He was a member of the Board of Trade and chairman of the Police and Licence boards, and from 1899 until 1904, he served as a Victoria alderman. In 1912, he was elected Victoria's twenty-seventh mayor and served in that position for a one-year term. During his term of office, a new reservoir was built at Smith's Hill and the Sooke Lake Waterworks agreement was signed. It was a time of prosperity for Victoria when many of the downtown streets were paved and street beautification was promoted. J.L. was also an active member of the Baptist church and helped organize a water application for the First Baptist Church at Douglas and Roderick streets in 1911.

Agnes Beckwith died in 1927 and J.L. moved to the "Willingdon Apartments" where he was taken care of by family members. He later moved into his club and died there in 1934. Both a street and a park in the High Quadra area are named for this enterprising gentleman.

Between the years 1927 and 1957, the house changed hands frequently. On one occasion it became a shelter for teens. Since 1957, the Beckwiths' family home on Fernwood has been a multi-dwelling residence.

Jean Vantreight was the first Beckwith grandchild and oldest daughter of J.L.'s son, Harold, and his wife Margaret Dunn. Harold became a lawyer and his wife Margaret was a teacher. Jean recalls her grandparents' home as being a warm, friendly house and, although she was still very young when they lived there, she remembers sitting upstairs and listening to their Edison gramophone playing music from the *The Mikado* and the song "Whistler and His Dog" which she particularly enjoyed.

Her grandparents had a Chinese cook named Wong whose English was somewhat limited. The kitchen was his territory which no one ever dared invade. On one occasion, as Jean was playing on the floor while the adults ate dinner, she discovered a lump in the carpet which was the bell that Agnes Beckwith pressed with her foot to summon Wong. Jean, not knowing what it was, was intrigued by the lump and kept pressing it at regular intervals. Each time, Wong would appear asking, "You ring, missy?" He was told no, so he left shaking his head. After about the third time of Wong's rushing into the dining room thinking he was urgently needed, the adults figured out what was happening.

Jean also remembered an enormous cherry tree in the backyard, and her grandfather's Buick in the garage with its large, carved, wooden, steering wheel. When the garage was not housing the Buick, neighbourhood children were allowed to play basketball there.

The importance of higher education continued through the generations and Jean became a teacher as did her sister, Sheila. Their brother John chose a musical career at the University of Toronto and subsequently became dean of music there and a world-renowned composer.

1423 Fernwood Road

FAIRFIELD HOUSE

A TRUTCH TREASURE

The ten-acre property which once surrounded elegant "Fairfield House" on Trutch Street was owned by Joseph and Julia Trutch. Their home was originally approached by a long driveway which today forms part of Collinson Street.

The exact date of the house's construction is unknown, but in 1861 Joseph Trutch purchased ten acres of land in the area which had originally formed part of James Douglas' Fairfield Farm. Trutch then built his home, designed by architects Wright and Sanders, on the rocky rise and described it as a "modest cottage, prettily situated."

The site chosen would certainly have been beautiful. Surrounding fields were full of purple, gold and white wildflowers growing in profusion, and cows and horses grazed under the trees in the cleared pastures. It was an idyllic location.

The Fairfield area in the 1860s and 1870s would have seemed a great distance away from the O'Reilly property on the Gorge Arm. Nonetheless, Fairfield House and Point Ellice House, and especially the two families who resided in these prestigious homes, were irrevocably connected. It was at one of the popular Trutch dinner parties held at Fairfield House that Joseph's sister, Caroline, met the dashing Peter O'Reilly who was a frequent dinner guest there. At the time, Caroline and her mother were visiting Joseph and Julia in Victoria, Caroline having already travelled to many places around the world. Quite possibly she and O'Reilly immediately fell in love in the pleasant Fairfield House ambience; their subsequent marriage united the two families forever. In the coming years, sisters-in-law Caroline O'Reilly and Julia Trutch became great friends and were two of the most prominent social chatelaines in early Victoria.

The Trutches had soon converted Fairfield House into a large, elegant home of importance, Julia enjoying playing social hostess to numerous guests through the years. Despite frequent trips back to Joseph's home in England, she always claimed that they were happiest at Fairfield House.

The large drawing-room was often the scene of balls when "crinolined belles stepped gracefully through quadrilles and minuets, but abhorred that new-fangled invention, the waltz...."

Joseph enjoyed spending time in his library where he delighted in the book-lined alcoves flanking each side of the enormous fireplace complete with a mantel of California redwood. In the hallway, a Spanish mahogany bannister rail bordered the staircase leading to the upper floor, with a magnificent stained-glass window of greens, reds and purples situated at the bend in the stairs. The entire house boasted eight fireplaces, twenty-eight doors, and thirty-six wide, expansive windows overlooking the gardens and fields with views stretching all the way to the rolling Sooke hills. There was said to be no finer view of the sunset in all Victoria than from the terrace that encircled Fairfield House.

Through the years, the modest little cottage had indeed turned into an elegant mansion. In 1864, Joseph Trutch even rented his home to Governor

601 Trutch Street

Kennedy for use as the vice-regal mansion while renovations were being undertaken at Cary Castle.

Joseph Trutch had originally come to the colony as surveyor general for British Columbia, and in 1871 was appointed the province's first lieutenant-governor. This meant the Trutches had to leave Fairfield House for a while and take up residence at Cary Castle. Here again, American-born Julia played hostess with an inborn charm and ease.

The Trutches by then were firmly cemented in the high society of early Victoria. Not only had Joseph's sister married Gold Commissioner O'Reilly, but in 1870, his brother John Trutch married Zoe Musgrave, Governor Musgrave's sister.

For Julia Trutch, however, a sadness overshadowed her life as she was unable to bear children. She nonetheless delighted in making Christmastime very special for all her nieces and nephews. Whether living in the vice-regal mansion, or in her own home in Fairfield, she organized the decorating of the home with evergreens and candles and encouraged the children to participate in musical festivities.

John and Zoe Trutch lived on the mainland for many years but also spent long sojourns at Fairfield House with the family. In 1885 they returned to the island and lived on Humboldt Street and then Richardson Street where, by 1890, they were sharing the same telephone number as Fairfield House. The Trutches were most certainly one of the first families to own the new-fangled telephone machine, and Fairfield House one of the first homes in which it was installed.

Joseph's term as lieutenant-governor ended in July of 1876, and he and Julia then left on an extended trip to England. The following year Joseph was knighted by the Queen, so it was as Sir Joseph and Lady Trutch that the couple returned once more to Fairfield House to enjoy their important new status. Trutch had been justly rewarded for his services to British Columbia.

Although by then he was wishing to retire and enjoy the pleasures of his home, it was not to be and soon Trutch found himself embroiled in the political question of the railway. He desperately wanted to be certain that all of the original terms of union were adhered to in order to ensure British Columbia's future. In 1880 he was rewarded by John A. Macdonald for his long service to the province with a prestigious appointment as B.C.'s adviser to the dominion government.

Retirement finally came in 1894, at which time Joseph and Julia were able to travel to England again. While away, Julia fell ill and craved to return to Fairfield House where she claimed she had always been happiest and felt confident her health would improve there. Sadly, improvement did not occur and she died the following July.

Joseph, now a lonely and depressed man, could not bear living at Fairfield House without his beloved Julia, so he returned once again to his homeland and spent the remainder of his life in Taunton, Somerset, until his death in March of 1904.

The sub-dividing of the Trutch estate in 1906 was the beginning of development in Fairfield which was later to become a major residential area in Victoria. Number 601 Trutch, although well-preserved, bears little resemblance to its grandeur as Fairfield House in that other era.

Renovations in the 1980s to a multi-dwelling home helped turn the house into an important part of the Trutch Street cluster of character homes.

Rockland Area

In the early 1880s architect Charles Vereydhen began to plan the layout of almost ten acres between Fort Street and today's Rockland Avenue (then known as Belcher Avenue). This area would eventually become known as Rockland. More building took place at the turn of the century and gradually the Rockland area became the domain of the rich and famous. As such, the most well-known and prestigious architects of the day were called upon by their wealthy clients to design many of the fine homes to be found there.

This area must indeed have been delightful. A young Nellie (Todd) Gillespie, whose family was considering building a house on Shasta Place in the area of St. Charles Street soon after the turn of the twentieth century, wrote a letter in 1903 to her older brother back east describing those Rockland delights.

> I think when you see it, you will be satisfied.... First it is a most beautiful situation, near to town, high splendid views and good air...the soil is very good, being rich and moist. There are some splendid oak trees and plenty of broom and scrub oak...and there is splendid rock foundation....
>
> I wish you could have seen it today as we did when standing on those rocks. The sun was shining on the buttercups and bright green grass, the trees budding out, the sea, the mountains, the hills, and the splendid, splendid air. Oh, it is good to live in such a place and on such a day!

Perhaps the most prominent building influence in the Rockland area can be seen today in the designs of architects Samuel Maclure, F.M. Rattenbury, P.L. James and John Wright. Most people, however, think of Rockland primarily as Maclure country.

The four homes chosen in this area tell varied stories: the first concerns one of the prominent Barnard family homes; another was the home built for Bank of British Columbia officials; the third is a pleasant white house tucked away off Rockland Avenue which was once party to a family's scandal; and the fourth was the home of a salmon-canning magnate's son.

1462 ROCKLAND AVENUE

DUVALS HOLDS MANY FAMILY MEMORIES

Originally known as "Duvals Cottage," 1462 Rockland Avenue was built in 1862 for Elizabeth Miles, the former owner of Cary Castle which once stood across the street from Duvals Cottage. Mrs. Miles subsequently sold the castle, which was Victoria's first Government House, to Governor Arthur Kennedy.

She did not own Duvals Cottage for very long either because by 1865 records show it had been sold yet again and was then occupied by the Honourable Sir Joseph Needham, chief justice of the Colony of Vancouver Island.

Yet another sale in 1870 placed this Victorian Gothic-revival cottage in the hands of the Barnard family. Francis Jones Barnard, owner of the once-famous Barnard Express Cariboo stage line, had purchased the house which was then destined to remain in the Barnard family for the next eighty-five years. During that time many significant events took place within its walls.

As the Barnard family added onto or renovated their home, and a second generation took over residence, the house was re-named simply "Duvals." By then, it had definitely outgrown its cottage status.

Today it is difficult to imagine this vastly altered house as once being the scene of many social functions, including balls and weddings, but the Barnard family were one of Victoria's early "jet-setters" and loved to entertain and show off their delightful home. They were also a family who had more than proved themselves through the generations to be both enterprising and spirited, and had easily infiltrated that inner sanctum of Victoria's elite establishment. Duvals was the perfect backdrop for their lavish lifestyle.

Frank Barnard senior was born in eastern Canada in 1829 and his descendants claimed a true Canadian heritage. After marriage to Ellen Stillman in 1853, he decided to head west in 1859 where prospects seemed better. By 1862, he had established his "pony express" which eventually became Barnard's Express, carrying both passengers and freight through canyons and across suspension bridges throughout the Cariboo. He soon controlled all the express services from Victoria to Barkerville.

Frank and Ellen raised three children in their home on Rockland Avenue, Francis (born in Toronto), and Alice and George Henry (Harry) born in Victoria. Over the coming decades, all three with their spouses either set up home in Duvals itself or were given land within the Duvals estate.

Eldest son Francis (Frank) joined his father in the family business and took over the reins completely when the senior Barnard suffered a stroke. He married Martha Loewen, daughter of Joseph Loewen, the owner of the Phoenix Brewing Company, in 1883. After their society wedding they returned to live in Duvals before eventually moving to a home known as "Clovelly" in Esquimalt overlooking Victoria harbour. Frank was also very politically minded and, in December of 1914, became British Columbia's lieutenant- governor. He and Martha then took up residence at Government House across from Duvals.

By that time, younger brother Harry and his wife, the former Ethel Rogers, were living at Duvals and remained there for the rest of their long and happy marriage, celebrating their golden wedding anniversary in the house in 1945.

Daughter Alice Barnard had also been given a slice of the Duvals estate when she married John Mara in 1882, their marriage having taken place in the drawing-room of Duvals. With a gown made of white corded silk and a long train embroidered and trimmed in satin and lace, Alice made a beautiful bride as she married her sweetheart. Mara's own life had been nothing less than adventurous, he being one of the famous "Overlanders" of 1862 who had travelled to British Columbia by an overland route. He remained in the province to prosper and rise in society, and his marriage to Alice Barnard was a high-society event in Victoria that year.

John and Alice Mara built their first home on the Duvals estate where they raised their two children, Lytton and Nellie. Both children also lived for many years on the original Barnard-owned property.

Politics and close proximity to the seat of government were always paramount in Barnard family life. Barnard senior, aside from his entrepreneurial attributes as owner of the Express stage coaches, had been a member of the B.C. Colonial Assembly and later an M.P. for Yale. Frank was M.P. for the Cariboo and later, of course, lieutenant-governor of the entire province, and Harry was also an M.P. and a senator. Son-in-law John Mara was for some time speaker of the B.C. legislature and later M.P. for Yale.

Despite their high political aspirations, one suspects the Barnard family were happiest when spending time together at Duvals. During those three generations of occupancy, the house changed its appearance considerably, eventually acquiring its high-pitched gables and country Gothic style of today. In addition, a porch was extended around the house on all sides and the balustrades ornamented with popular Victorian gingerbread. In 1911, architects James & James again enlarged the house to its current proportions.

Since the 1950s, the one-time family-oriented home has been the Mary Manor Apartments. Situated across from present-day Government House, it is still in close proximity to the political arena of today, its inner voice perhaps recalling similar political events during the time the Barnards were in residence.

1462 Rockland Avenue

HIGHWOOD

THE BANKERS' HOUSE

William Curtis Ward who was born in Winchester, England, in 1843, arrived on Vancouver Island in 1864 with his eighteen-year-old bride, Lydia Sothcott. He had been transferred to the Victoria branch of the original Bank of British Columbia to take up a position as accountant there. Within two years of his arrival, he was promoted to manager.

Three years later, the bank built a prestigious house known as "Highwood" in the Rockland area for their manager. It was destined to become the official residence for all their future banking officers. In its day, it was a large, elegant home surrounded by five acres of land between Rockland Avenue and Fort Street.

Just as William Ward himself played a large part in the history of Victoria, so did the bank for whom he worked play a role in the development of the entire province. When, for instance, the bank refused to extend more credit to the colonial government in 1866, their wise decision encouraged the union of the colonies of Vancouver Island and British Columbia, and subsequently this same decision led to British Columbia entering Confederation in 1871.

Under the management of William Ward, the bank prospered, and his Rockland home became the scene of many social functions with Lydia acting as hostess. The couple raised six daughters and five sons, so a large house was very appropriate to their needs.

William took an active interest both in the community around him and in his church, Christ Church Cathedral, where he was appointed rector's warden in 1872 and 1874, and people's warden in 1877 and 1881. He was also president of the Board of Trade from 1899 to 1901 and, together with a number of other prominent men in the city, strongly encouraged the game of rugby football in 1885.

While not entertaining at Highwood, involved in banking affairs, or actively working on his many other interests, he was involved in various other business matters. In 1884, he established the Douglas Lake Cattle Company as one of its founding members. This company grew considerably with the acquisition of more cattle and grazing lands to become the largest cattle ranch in Canada by the end of the Second World War. In 1910, Ward bought out his other two partners in the Douglas Lake Company and established his son, Frank, as manager. Each of his children was later given equal shares in the ranch when, in 1950, it was sold to Victor Spencer (of Spencer's Stores) and Frank McKenzie Ross (lieutenant-governor of B.C. in the 1950s).

The Ward family left Canada in 1897 to return to England, but at the beginning of the First World War decided to come back to the relative safety of Canada. They then settled in another large house (no longer in existence) on Shasta Place off St. Charles Street.

Meanwhile, in 1901, the Bank of British Columbia had been bought out by the Canadian Imperial Bank of Commerce and was then situated at Bastion and Government streets. The man who took over management of the newly

1021 Gillespie Place

established branch was George Gillespie who moved his family into Highwood. Gillespie Place was subsequently named for this gentleman. In 1921, one of George Gillespie's sons, Erroll, married Catharine Oliver, a granddaughter of William Curtis Ward, thereby joining the two banking families in marriage as well as in residence.

As a point of interest, one of the Bank of British Columbia's best known employees was undoubtedly Robert W. Service, the Canadian poet of Yukon fame, who joined the bank in 1903 at a salary of $50 and while employed in Victoria lived in accommodation above the bank vault. He was later transferred to the Kamloops branch and ultimately to Whitehorse.

Highwood, the solid masonry house that prestigious banking families had made their home for decades, is believed to have been designed by John Teague. It bears a resemblance to the "Admiral's House" built by Teague at the naval dockyard sixteen years later. In 1890, extensive improvements and alterations were made to the banking house, including the addition of the front bay windows.

Today, the imposing "Bankers' House" is situated behind a high fence at the top end of Gillespie Place off Rockland Avenue and is one of the oldest houses in the Rockland area.

FAIRHOLME

THE HOUSE WHICH HELD A FAMILY SECRET

Tucked away on Rockland Place, an offshoot of Rockland Avenue near its intersection with St. Charles Street, sits an interesting house built for Dr. John Chapman Davie by contractors Hill and Conley in 1886. It is believed to have been designed by architect John Teague.

This white, Italianate home was constructed for the sum of $7,000 in a style popular with professional men towards the end of the nineteenth century. Its bay windows and balconied porch were features many homes shared at that time. Dr. Davie's house, however, held a secret precipitated by a scandal involving the prominent Jacob Hunter Todd family.

On a visit to Duncan in March of 1876, the then-very-married father of three daughters, John Davie, had met the charming, twenty-one-year-old Sara Holmes Todd, eldest daughter of Jacob Hunter Todd. He was enchanted with her, and they began to meet frequently at various social events in the months that followed. Needless to say, Sara's very proper and circumspect father strongly disapproved of his headstrong and somewhat rebellious daughter's relationship with a married man and tried desperately to discourage it.

In point of fact, until Davie's passion for Sara took over and obsessed his life, the doctor had been considered a highly professional, well-respected man in Victoria. He was the youngest of the four sons of Dr. J.C. Davie, senior, and had arrived on Vancouver Island with his family in 1862 as a young man of seventeen. He began medical training in San Francisco and, once qualified, became a well-loved doctor in Victoria like his father before him. He was largely responsible for the design of the first Jubilee Hospital and was an early promoter of Lord Lister's antiseptic surgical methods. He performed many innovative, far- ahead-of-their-time operations at the Jubilee Hospital.

Davie courted Sara Todd for some years before his wife's death, which some said occurred as a result of a broken heart – she having known of his clandestine involvement with Sara. He finally married Sara in 1884 at St. Peter's Church in Quamichan. When news of the marriage reached Jacob Todd, he was devastated. His own strict moral upbringing did not allow him to accept his daughter's relationship with this man even though Davie's first wife had now passed away and Davie and Sara had legitimized their union. Todd was so incensed by the scandal that he vowed to have nothing more to do with his daughter. Members of the Todd family today believe that he even cut her out of his will; however, it appears Todd's final will and codicil did allow Sara a portion of his estate to be "held by trustees."

Despite Sara's father's disapproval, Dr. Davie gave orders in 1885 for the building of "Fairholme" on Rockland Hill. The house was to overlook the Pemberton meadows out towards the sea and the mountains. The couple, with Davie's three daughters to whom Sara had become a devoted stepmother, moved in by 1886. She found happiness and contentment in their pleasant Italianate home and, despite lacking any social contact with her estranged family, was compensated by the companionship and love of her husband's daughters for whom she enjoyed arranging tennis parties on the lawns. Rare family photographs showed Sara on the manicured lawns acting as hostess at these social events. She loved to entertain and soon her home became a popular site for elegant soirees. It would appear that Sara Todd Davie became an accepted member of high society despite the scandal which had surrounded her marriage.

In April of 1893, the first of her stepdaughters, Maud, was married from Fairholme to William A. Ward of Robert Ward & Company. After an elaborate wedding at Christ Church Cathedral, guests were invited back to the family home for the reception.

Less than one year later, Sara, at the young age of thirty-nine, lay dying of pneumonia – not even her husband's great medical skills could save her. On July 16, 1894, Sara died, still not reconciled with her father, who was to live on for another five years.

Although separated from most of her family for many years, it seems that her older brother Charles had kept at least minimal contact with her during her ten-year marriage to the doctor. He retained photographs taken at Fairholme of Sara as reminders of her happier years. He also possessed a photograph of her grave covered in many floral tributes after her elaborate funeral service. With a touch of irony, Sara was laid to rest at Ross Bay Cemetery in a grave alongside Kate Thain, the first Mrs. John Chapman Davie.

Although Dr. Davie himself survived until 1911, he remained faithful to the memory of his beloved Sara despite rumours to the contrary. For a short time, he had traded his respectable reputation for the passion he felt for Sara, and had then poured all his love for her into the building of this elegant Rockland home.

This well-preserved building today goes by the name of Fairholme Manor. It is an attractive and popular bed-and-breakfast establishment offering many delights from the Victorian era, including the echoes of a scandal which once rocked respectable Victoria.

638 Rockland Place

ILLAHIE

THE MAGIC OF ANOTHER ERA

It was the kind of home only the rich could afford in the early years of the twentieth century. "Illahie" is the Samuel Maclure masterpiece situated on the corner of St. Charles and Maud streets in one of Victoria's most prestigious areas.

Houses such as Illahie were built for people of prominence. Elizabethan in design, its gables, bay windows, and brick-ribbed chimneys are perfectly suited to its original owner, Charles Fox Todd, an important industrialist in early British Columbia.

It is the entrance hall of Illahie, however, which makes the final and absolute statement about Todd the man. Although he was very wealthy, Todd's tastes were basically simple. Nonetheless, in his entrance hall he indulged in excessive displays of wealth such as the mother-of-pearl inlay in the newel post of the magnificent staircase. Alongside is an elaborate stained-glass window designed by McCausland & Company of Toronto. Entitled "Spring," the window shows a woman tending her garden and is captioned with the opening lines of "Cherry Ripe" by poet Thomas Campion:

There is a Garden in Her Face
Where roses and white lilies grow.

Light filtering through the window's myriad colours creates both elegance and an awesome, church-like atmosphere. The window is a strong departure from the otherwise orthodox life of this strict businessman.

Charles Fox Todd (known always as "Charlie") was the son of Jacob Hunter Todd and Anna Fox, and was born in Brampton, Ontario, in 1856, a year after his sister, Sara.

Jacob had headed west in 1862 to establish himself as a merchant of note in both Victoria and Barkerville, while Charlie and Sara were sent to the best schools in eastern Canada. At age nineteen Charlie returned to Victoria and became apprenticed to his father. By the time he was twenty-one he was a partner in the family business, J.H. Todd & Son. After Anna Fox died, Jacob married Rosanna Wigley and began raising a second family. He also took more interest in politics. Consequently, most of the business responsibilities were left to young Charlie.

By 1881, the Todds were becoming interested in the canning industry. They initially entered this lucrative business as agents for two canneries, but soon decided to buy their own cannery in Richmond. Once they had registered their Horseshoe brand with its catchy phrase "The Pick of the Pacific," there was no looking back. The Todd enterprise gradually grew into an empire.

When Jacob Todd died in 1899, Charlie took over the reins and the business continued to grow. Soon many hundreds of families throughout British Columbia were gaining a living through Todd canneries and their large-scale commercial fish-trap operations. Their Sooke fish traps operated until the 1950s.

1041 St. Charles Street

Charlie was also a family man and he and his wife Louisa raised two sons, William and Ernest. Charlie liked to be surrounded by his family and, in later years, always invited his grandchildren for breakfast with him on Sunday at Illahie where Chu, the Chinese cook, served pancakes, sausage and eggs. Then they would all ride together at Willows Academy. On other occasions, the children were allowed to play in the upstairs attic with the multitude of toys kept there that included skipping ropes, scooters, wagons, a pedal airplane and roller skates.

Christmas at Illahie was a very special time. A large tree was placed in the front hall at the foot of the winding staircase surrounded by presents. Charlie was especially generous to his grandchildren. Throughout the year he also supplied them with pocket money, either a $5 gold piece or a $5 bill, a veritable fortune in those times.

But Charlie was also something of an enigma. His generous nature at home did not extend to outsiders, especially if he felt he was being used, and he resented people who took advantage of his generosity.

During the First World War he was decorated by the French government with a medal and the Diploma of Honor in recognition of his services to the Allied cause. He also served for many years on the Royal Jubilee Hospital's board of directors, and made numerous donations including x-ray equipment to both the Royal Jubilee and St. Joseph's hospitals in memory of his wife Louisa Todd.

His connection with the Victoria Golf Club is also noteworthy. He initially purchased the property from the James Dunsmuir estate, then gave the golf links to the Victoria Golf Club members, retaining a mortgage on the property.

On one occasion a burglar tried to gain entry to Illahie but was spotted by a neighbour who called the police. The burglar hid in an upstairs bathroom and when a police officer fired through the door he was hit in the leg and surrendered. One of Charlie's grandsons claims that Charlie then gave the intruder "the worst tongue-licking imaginable!"

Todd's descendants are not sure why their ancestor chose the name Illahie for his home. In Chinook the word translates as "land," "property" or even "earth." Today we might express this as meaning real estate. Charlie frequently worked alongside the native Indians and always enjoyed their language, so he may well have been impressed with the pleasant-sounding word "illahie" and used it to describe his prime piece of real estate where everyone was always made welcome.

Ninety-four years after it was built, Charlie Todd's grand mansion on St. Charles Street is an exclusive apartment house, but still retains the magic of another era.

Esquimalt

Esquimalt is the Anglicized pronunciation of the native Indian word "es-whoy-malth," which means "a shoaling place." Situated "beyond the blue bridge" to the west of Victoria it comprises approximately 1,006 hectares of land and another 374 hectares of water, and today has a population of around 17,000.

Development began in the area after James Douglas had first seen Esquimalt's agricultural potential. He then established three farms (Viewfield, Craigflower and Constance Cove) to be controlled by the Puget's Sound Agricultural Company, a subsidiary of the Hudson's Bay Company. Because Esquimalt possessed one of the finest natural harbours on the west coast, the Royal Navy had also seen the area's great potential in the 1840s and 1850s and frequently used the harbour for its own purposes. This continued for many decades. By 1887, a naval dockyard was completed which enabled the Royal Navy to repair and refit ships on Canadian soil.

A small village of homes had grown up there in 1855, and by 1858 it had increased to accommodate the prospectors en route to Victoria and ultimately the goldfields. In the following years, development continued, both in the village and along the Esquimalt Road, a road which began as a rough native Indian trail, too precarious for many to travel.

As Victoria's population grew and the naval presence in Esquimalt dominated the area's social life, many of the city's wealthy decided to build their homes in Esquimalt with the most popular areas being along the shoreline, along the banks of the Gorge Arm, or on the rocky sites of Old Esquimalt Road. The old naval base was abandoned by the Royal Navy in 1905 to make way for the newly created Royal Canadian Navy in 1910.

By the time Esquimalt was incorporated in 1912, the landscape had greatly changed, but many of the old heritage homes remained and do to this day. The following stories include tales of some majestic homes on Old Esquimalt Road, as well as the story of the home of an old sea captain, that of a reputed hermit and the tale of a house steeped in rumours of espionage during the First World War.

THE CAPTAIN'S HOUSE

BUILT FOUR-SQUARE TO COMPASS

The steamboat Gothic-style house on Head Street in Esquimalt has been a familiar landmark in that area since it was built in 1893 by Captain Victor Jacobson.

The house was built to Jacobson's own specifications which accounts for many of its unusual touches such as the carved woodwork representing the butterflies, flowers, and birds which his wife loved so much, alongside the stars, anchors and ropes depicting his own seafaring life. The tower on top of the house was added so that he could look out across the water to watch for the return of his sealing fleet.

Much of the house, including the mansard roof, is faced with fish-scales, and other decorative shingles. Although unusual in design, Jacobson's house was built the way he wanted it to look, with profits made from seal hunting.

The captain's real name was Vicktor Jackob Holmlund and he was born in Finland in 1852. Shortly after arriving in Canada, he changed his name to Vicktor Jackobson and then later dropped both "k's." At age thirteen he was forced to become the family breadwinner so he went to sea to earn a living as a cook's helper. For the next five years he sailed the world.

In 1880 he arrived in Victoria aboard the *City of Quebec,* decided he liked this part of the world and wanted to stay. His captain refused to allow him to "jump ship" but Victor had other ideas, so he dived overboard, swam ashore, and eventually found work on a farm in the "wilds of Saanich."

He later worked as a carpenter for a Captain Spring who operated trading stations on the west coast of Vancouver Island. However, an early voyage aboard a sealing schooner, the *Mary Ellen*, convinced him that he wanted to resume his love affair with the sea.

Sealing was a profitable business for him and he soon made a considerable amount of money. On one visit to Victoria between voyages, he decided to look around for a boat of his own. He found a small schooner, the *Mountain Chief,* which was sunk in mud beneath the old James Bay Bridge. Once he had located her owner, he made an offer of $400, fixed her up, and went into business for himself. The rest was history.

Over the next few years, Jacobson found great success as a seal hunter. Following his marriage in 1888 to Minnie McLean, he purchased a second schooner, named it the *Minnie*, and continued to have many more adventures at sea, most of which were later chronicled in a series of articles written in the 1960s by his daughter, Mrs. E.M. Sweeney.

By the 1890s and now with a growing family, Jacobson decided to purchase acreage in Esquimalt where he built his steamboat Gothic house. Even though he had built the house close to the water with a wide view of the harbour, he soon discovered that he much preferred to live on the water rather than alongside it. With this in mind, he purchased an old sternwheeler, the *Distributor*, which had once been in service on the Skeena, and this became his second home floating in front of his "Big House." As his wife worked in the galley of the sternwheeler, she was happy in the knowledge that the captain could still feel the swell beneath him as he slept.

The Big House was never empty, though. Jacobson sent for his seventy-year-old mother who arrived with a sixteen-year-old granddaughter, Svea Peterson. Old Mrs. Holmlund spoke only Swedish and encouraged all her grandchildren to learn to speak that language. Although they were Finnish by birth, part of Finland was controlled by Sweden at that time, hence the Swedish language being Mrs. Holmlund's mother tongue. She always kept a cow, a horse, and a few chickens on the Head Street property, and could often be seen fishing from her old rowboat. She lived to the age of ninety-six.

Minnie Jacobson died in 1942, and the old sea captain moved to Vancouver to be with one of his daughters while his son, Victor, kept up the home on Head Street. Captain Jacobson passed away at age ninety-seven, still telling stories of his bold adventures hunting seals in the Bering Sea and North Pacific.

The distinctive house on Head Street remained in the Jacobson family until the 1950s. The old *Distributor* however, continued to gather barnacles and was eventually abandoned and broken up, thus ending a colourful era in the history of sternwheelers.

By the 1960s, the Big House itself was also in a sad state of disrepair, but in 1963 it was purchased by Gil and Marguerite Laurensen who injected life back into the old sealing skipper's house, managing to retain all of its late-Victorian-era uniqueness.

Although no longer owned by the Laurensens, the Jacobson house continues to be an important Esquimalt landmark. In January 1998, despite some opposition from those who considered "sealing" to be a less than honourable profession and politically incorrect in today's world, the Esquimalt municipality agreed to honour the old sea captain by renaming West Bay Park in Esquimalt, "Captain Jacobson Park."

Together with his landmark house, the park has become a fitting memorial to a colourful character in Victoria's history.

507 Head Street

TYN-Y-COED and VIEWFIELD HOUSE

AN OGILVIE-PRICE CONNECTION

The Queen Anne-style house known as "Tyn-Y-Coed" at 820 Dunsmuir Road and the one known as "Viewfield House" at 1024 Munro have an interesting connection.

Hans Ogilvie-Price, who designed the Macaulay Point Golf Course (the oldest golf course in British Columbia, when it finally closed in the 1940s), and also worked as a clerk at the naval dockyard, purchased the Dunsmuir Road property in 1900. Street directories, however, state that he and his family had lived there since 1895, the time the house was built.

Ogilvie-Price also purchased land in the vicinity of Munro Street and Pooley Place, and at about the same time had Viewfield House built as a rental property. His intention in building a second house was to give employment to a family friend, an architect who had recently arrived from England.

Soon after the turn of the century, Ogilvie-Price died, and in 1907 his wife and daughter, Frances, moved to England. When they returned to Victoria in 1910, tenants were then occupying their Dunsmuir Road house, so mother and daughter moved into the vacant Munro Street house.

Mrs. Price wished the house to remain exactly as her husband had built it and would not concede to any alterations or improvements through the years. She did, however, finally agree to update the central heating by having a large coal heater placed in the hall but she insisted on having it cleaned, dismantled and put away in storage every summer. A Chinese cook occupied a small room off the back porch and took care of the house.

Mrs. Price later married again, this time to Major George Sizman. After Mrs. Price's death in 1951, the major and Frances left Viewfield House and moved to Oak Bay. Major Sizman lived well into his nineties, celebrating a life which had included service with the Royal Canadian Artillery at Work Point Barracks, helping to re-organize the Macaulay Point Golf Club in the early 1920s, and serving as people's warden at St. Paul's and Garrison Church for twenty-seven years. He was also an ardent fly-fisherman in his younger days.

Born in Dorset, England, Sizman had enlisted in the Royal Garrison Artillery in 1894 and in 1895 had left London for service in Bermuda. He then moved to Halifax in 1897. In March of 1906 he was named deputy assistant adjutant and quartermaster general for Military District II at Work Point when the garrison was taken over from the Imperial Army. Sizman was called back to active duty during the Second World War for two more years of service.

Meanwhile, the house he had shared as Mrs. Price's second husband on Munro Street was destined to have five more owners through the years, until 1982 when it was purchased by the Terry family. By then, previous owners had allowed the house to become run down and the grounds overgrown.

The Terrys then took on the mammoth task of restoring the house after decades of neglect. Linoleum and carpet covered the original wood floors and

1024 Munro Street

there were also ceilings that had been lowered and windows walled in. On some of the walls, they discovered six layers of wallpaper. The original mantelpieces and tiles had also been stripped by a previous owner.

Gradually the Terrys managed to restore the house to its previous glory. Turn-of-the-century light fixtures were added, as well as an addition to accommodate a bed-and-breakfast which they ran for five years.

The house was later turned into a legal duplex, but the Terrys themselves still live in the original part of Viewfield and retain it as it once was. The doors of the old house were duplicated and custom-made wainscoting was installed throughout. The old woodshed on the property has been converted to a computer room, and Victorian-type furniture has been added throughout the house, from the Terrys' own collection, to give it a warm and authentic ambience.

Meanwhile, the other Ogilvie-Price house of note at 820 Dunsmuir still stands, but with little alteration through the years except for a solar collector added on the south side. Stained-glass windows adorn the second floor above the front door. As a point of interest, during the 1950s, the Canadian writer, Margaret Laurence, was an owner of this property.

820 Dunsmuir Road

TRAFALGAR

THE COTTON HOUSE

Since Victoria architect, Peter Neve Cotton, acquired this stately home on Admirals Road in 1970, and set about renovating and beautifying it before his death in 1979, it has been popularly referred to as the "Cotton House."

Its original name, however, was most probably "Trafalgar," although there are some who claim it may also have held the name "Gibraltar" at one time. What is known with certainty is that this rambling, old landmark edifice, standing like a bastion on the rise in Admirals Road and overlooking Esquimalt Harbour and the Sooke hills, was built in 1900 for the Reverend William Bolton and his wife, Agnes (Bushby).

Bolton was the founding principal of University School which is now known as St. Michael's University School, and his wife was a granddaughter of Sir James Douglas. The evolution of title to the land on which Trafalgar was built, dates back to the year 1857 when it was owned by James Douglas, and passed through such familiar names as Thomas Trounce and Thomas Dodds, before the house was actually built in 1900.

Equally well-known owners of this grand home were the Reverend Reginald Walker and his wife, Lady Emily, daughter of Lord Hereford, in the 1930s. Lady Emily was a descendant of Lady Jane Seymour, the third wife of King Henry VIII, and she enjoyed entertaining many important people both at Trafalgar and at her East Sooke home, "Ragley," where the Prince of Wales (later Edward VIII) was once a guest.

The late historian, James K. Nesbitt, claimed that as a young farm-page editor, he always covered the fall fairs in Sooke and remembered Lady Emily "in all her glory, working like a beaver, displaying her farm produce, her fingers asparkle with rings of diamonds, emeralds and rubies...a diamond sunburst on her coveralls; sometimes she even wore a tiara."

Lady Emily was apparently a very public-spirited lady who did much good in her community. She died in 1948 at the age of seventy-five and is buried in the little churchyard of St. Mary's at Metchosin.

Another occupant of the house on Admirals Road was Commodore Walter Hose who brought the HMCS *Rainbow* to Esquimalt in 1911, and lived at Trafalgar while stationed here. He was the son of the bishop of Singapore and was born at sea in the Indian Ocean in 1875 aboard the P.& O. Steamship *Surat.* He joined the British navy at age fifteen and by 1928 had risen to the rank of rear-admiral. He died in Ontario in 1965 when almost ninety years old, and a plaque at St. Paul's Church in Esquimalt honours him today. The plaque was presented and dedicated in 1967 by officers and men of the HMCS *Malahat.*

Peter Cotton was, of course, the best-known owner of the house. He acquired heritage designation for his excellent restoration work of the building, and was also remembered for the extensive part he played in the restoration of other sites around town such as Carr House, Craigflower Manor, the Law Chambers, and the Counting House. He was also involved in the exterior restoration of St. Andrew's Cathedral and many of his papers, drawings and plans are held in the British Columbia archives.

Born in Merritt in 1918, Cotton grew up in New Westminster. During the Second World War he served overseas in British Army Intelligence and attained the rank of captain. After the war he pursued his architectural studies at the University of British Columbia, attended the Massachusetts Institute of Technology, and later studied art history at the University of Victoria. During his career, he designed and manufactured furniture in his own Vancouver factory, and then took a position with the provincial government to work on the rebuilding of Government House after the fire there in 1957. He also worked with Cool-Aid, a society which has its origins in the Cool Aid Hostel established in 1968 to provide short-term emergency shelter for transient youth, and today offers a wide range of social services within the community. Cotton's interest in theatricals also led him into helping to convert the old Baptist Church on Fernwood Street into today's Belfry Theatre.

Although Trafalgar is no longer a single-family dwelling, this three-storey colonial- type structure with its intriguing dormers and verandas has managed to retain its heritage ambience as six strata units. Its fascinating past and especially its interesting past owners have each, in their own way, contributed to Trafalgar's charm as a unique Esquimalt landmark.

639 Admirals Road

1211 OLD ESQUIMALT ROAD

AN EXPLOSIVE HOUSE

Described as the second-oldest house on the street, "Longstone," at 1211 Old Esquimalt Road, is an interesting structure built for a man who led a fascinating life. Thought to have been designed by Samuel Maclure because of the many Maclure touches throughout, this grand old home was built in 1910 for Colonel John Albert Hall and his wife Annie.

In springtime, the lawns at Longstone are a sea of purple shooting-stars that delight the neighbourhood and passers-by, and continue to make the old house stand out and pique the curiosity of many people.

John Hall was born in Manchester, England, in 1868, graduated with distinction from Owen's College, Ontario, in 1888, and went to work for the Clayton Aniline Company until 1893. During those five years, he also earned his Master of Science degree.

That same year, Hall and a friend started the Victoria Chemical Company which later became known as Canadian Explosives. Hall acted as chief research chemist with the company until his retirement, but then continued to work on research in his own laboratory in Esquimalt.

In 1900, Hall began his military career as a junior officer in the Fifth Regiment and rose to become commanding officer in 1905. He held this position until 1908 when he began to organize the 88th Fusiliers. His love for military affairs led him to be placed in command of the Civil Aid Forces in 1913. This organization was formed in order to control the rioting taking place among colliery workers in the mines on Vancouver Island. Their headquarters were located in Nanaimo.

At the outbreak of war in 1914, Hall was active in the field of recruitment, but the following year he was sent overseas in command of the 30th Battalion which had by then incorporated with the 88th Fusiliers. The Halls were then living at Longstone.

After serving in France for a while, Hall was summoned by the War Office for special duty in connection with the manufacture of munitions: his area of expertise. After the First World War, he received an honorary degree from the University of Manchester, and soon afterward retired to settle once more in Esquimalt.

John Hall's work in the field of research covered salts of phosphoric, arsenic and vanadic acids, and in 1887 his findings were published in *Transactions,* a noted scientific publication. He was made a fellow of the Chemical Society in 1889.

Hall was also something of a car buff in the early days of the automobile. The garage on the property still has the pit beneath it where Hall enjoyed working on his cars. He died on May 18, 1932.

The house and its original large surrounding acreage were eventually sold to the Macallans. Two lots below the property were then subdivided. The house was also rented for a while, but since 1964 has been owned by the O'Malias.

1211 Old Esquimalt Road

1165 OLD ESQUIMALT ROAD

AN ESQUIMALT GEM

Strolling along Old Esquimalt Road today, one is treated to a myriad of charming homes varying in architectural style, size, age, and historical importance. Number 1165 is a case in point.

When it was built in 1913 for Ralph and Martha Stephens, instructions were given to the contractor for the materials used in the house to be equal to those used in the house of Tom Hawkins. This gentleman lived on Princess Avenue and was the owner of the general store known as Hawkins and Hayward at 1607 Douglas Street. He was also married to Martha Stephens' sister and his home was obviously of high quality. The Stephens wanted their home to be built with an equally high degree of workmanship, and were perhaps displaying a case of "keeping up with the Hawkins."

According to the current owners of number 1165, Sherri and Darwin Robinson, many of the light fixtures in the house are vintage 1880s and came from Tom Hawkins' store.

Sherri Robinson, a history buff who dedicates much of her time to volunteer work at the Esquimalt Archives, has also written a book on the street names of Esquimalt, while delving into the history of her own house in her spare time.

In her research, she discovered that a carpenter by the name of W. Benson, assisted by a Mr. McCrimmon, worked on 1165, and that the house was built a few months before the Percival Ridout Brown house, originally known as "Lyndhurst." This elegant home once stood directly across the street from 1165, but now, with other homes surrounding it, is situated on the off-shoot road called Warder Place. Today, Lyndhurst is better known as the "Pooley House."

Robert H. Pooley, son of Charles E. Pooley, purchased Lyndhurst in 1928. It remains the most prominent house in the area and was given heritage designation in 1985. Pooley senior lived at "Fernhill" (demolished in 1932) on the corner of Lampson and Old Esquimalt roads. Pooley owned a great deal of land along Old Esquimalt Road, including the land on which 1165 was built.

Ralph Stephens was an engineer who worked as foreman/machinist with the B.C. Marine Railway Co. Ltd., and stayed on with the shipyard when Yarrows took over in 1914. He and his wife lived at 1165 until his death in 1936. During those years, he befriended his neighbour, Robert Pooley, and on one occasion, during Pooley's term as attorney-general of British Columbia, the two friends had morning coffee together at 1165.

After coffee that day, Pooley left to attend a meeting, but forgot his briefcase. Suddenly remembering it, he hurriedly returned only to discover that everyone had gone out and the house was locked up. Desperately needing his papers and notes for the meeting, he could see only one option open to him. Without a second thought, he broke a window and entered through the back porch to retrieve his briefcase. The house, therefore, has the dubious distinction of being the only one ever broken into by an attorney-general of British Columbia!

1165 Old Esquimalt Road

Subsequent owners of 1165 were William J. Gibson who lived there until 1940, and the John Houghton family until 1944. George Douglas Cramb and his wife, Lillian, purchased the house that year. Cramb was a naval architect and marine engineer who had trained in England. He worked as assistant manager at Yarrows until 1944 when he retired and moved to the Old Esquimalt Road house. His wife had been accustomed to a luxurious home in Toronto and thought that the plumbing was rather primitive at 1165. She particularly disliked "the tub on legs and the pedestal sink" upstairs, so in the late 1940s a new built-in tub and sink replaced the old ones, and plastic tiles were added everywhere as was fashionable during the 1940s. Mr. Cramb remained in the house until 1984, and it was his second wife, Elizabeth, who sold the house to the Robinsons in January of 1985.

Since then, the back porch which had become infested with bugs has been replaced, and the lumber saved was recycled to create a built-in sideboard in the dining room and cupboards in the kitchen. Everything else in the house, barring the upstairs bathroom, is original. Character touches throughout the house include a dumbwaiter, a built-in ironing board, a linen cupboard with place for a hot iron, an old-fashioned kitchen clothes drying rack, a grounding aerial for a "wireless," fireplaces with covers and the original call bell system for the maid. Soon after moving in, the Robinson children were disappointed to discover that *their* mother was not a maid – she did not answer the call bell.

1165 Old Esquimalt Road does not appear ever to have had a name, and the Robinsons have toyed with the idea of calling it "Derryquin," the name of an estate in Ireland belonging to an ancestor of Sherri Robinson.

The exterior facade of 1165 is attractive with a recessed balcony on the second floor and two diamond-shaped windows on either side, similar to ones found on the house at 1010 Arcadia Street, the story of which follows. The distinctive monkey puzzle tree in the front garden of number 1165 was planted by the Stephens family back in 1913, and gives added appeal to this Esquimalt gem.

THE VON ALVENSLEBEN HOUSE

SPIES IN OUR MIDST?

A year after 1165 Old Esquimalt Road, the house at 1010 Arcadia Street was built for Werner (Bodo) and Fernandine Theodora Herberta Maria von Alvensleben. Quite possibly the same contractor was involved as the houses show similarities, especially in the use of the diamond-shaped windows on either side of the upper balcony.

The story of the Arcadia Street house, however, is a very different one. Even before the beginning of the First World War, there were rumours concerning the residents of the house, for Bodo Alvensleben was the brother of well-known Vancouver financier, Alvo von Alvensleben, who had made his fortune in the Vancouver real estate boom and had declared on more than one occasion that, as a proud Prussian, he was prepared "to die for the Fatherland."

Bodo by then was in charge of the Victoria branch of the Alvensleben Canadian Finance and General Investment Company, one of many companies in which the brothers were involved, but a few days after the outbreak of war he left somewhat hurriedly to join up. Wild rumours continued to dog the brothers as to their spying activities. One such rumour stated that Bodo was taken from his ship by a British man-of-war and, when searched, was found to have in his possession the plans of the Esquimalt naval yard, and that he was subsequently shot as a spy. Brother Alvo vehemently denied this rumour but the truth has never been discovered.

Another report, however, stated that Bodo simply left Canada for Germany, and was last heard of in 1933 when he was arrested in Berlin and charged by Hitler with high treason following two attempted assassinations. He supposedly was cleared of both charges.

Most of the activities of these two famous brothers are still on record, but many are contradictory and one is left wondering what roles the von Alvensleben brothers did in fact play in espionage, if any, once war was declared on Germany. Were any spying activities planned in Bodo's house on Arcadia Street or at Alvo's house at Forty-First and Blenheim in Vancouver?

The von Alvensleben story began in Prussia on the family estate in Westphalia. Alvo was the second son of Count Werner Alvo von Alvensleben, the German ambassador to Russia when Nicholas was still Czar. He was born in 1877 and grew up enjoying the good life. In 1904, however, against his father's wishes, he resigned his commission as a lieutenant and decided to explore the world. One story maintains that having gambled away his allowance and sowed more than his share of wild oats, he was cast out of the family by the senior von Alvensleben. Alvo's pride was hurt because he disliked no longer being a part of the elite circle which had included Kaiser Wilhelm, an intimate friend of his father's.

Nonetheless, Alvo set off on his adventures and arrived in Vancouver in 1904 with only $4 in his pocket. He lived for a while in an abandoned shack near a cannery at the mouth of the Fraser River. The *Canadian Courier* later headlined an article about him, "Hobo to Millionaire," because his lifestyle from then on was indeed a rags-to-riches story.

Knowing very little English, this tall, proud Prussian had a violent temper and was often unreasonable. He did eventually buckle down, after having led a playboy's life, and went to work whitewashing a salmon cannery, shooting ducks at 35 cents a head, and fishing salmon. He supplied the exclusive Vancouver Club with fish and game at their back door. A few years later, when he had become a very rich man and was nominated for membership in the exclusive club, he admitted to the head waiter, who had been staring at him while serving dinner, that he was indeed the man "who used to sell you people chickens at the back door!" He then added, "Now go on serving dinner and stop staring."

By 1909, Alvo's brother, Bodo, had joined him in Canada and the two men became involved in advertising and selling real estate. There were many opportunities for investors at that time as these were the boom years for Vancouver and money could easily be made.

Alvo had married Edith May Westcott, daughter of a Vancouver contractor, a year earlier, and had bought a ten-acre estate in Kerrisdale. There they had thirteen servants and entertained lavishly. As a remarkably talented wheeler-dealer, he organized the German-British Columbia Syndicate responsible for numerous German investments being made in western North America (including those of Kaiser Wilhelm, into whose good graces Alvo had now returned). One of Alvo's many investments was the once famous Wigwam Inn on Indian Arm and another was the Dominion Trust Building on West Hastings Street which was to become a landmark in the city of Vancouver.

When war was declared, however, Alvo von Alvensleben was in Berlin on business and, as an enemy alien, he could not return to Canada. His possessions here were seized by the government and rumours continued to circulate about the previous activities of the two brothers. Alvo maintained that such stories were "all nonsense, scandalous falsehoods," and eventually he returned to the United States (which remained neutral until 1917) to take up residence in Seattle.

When America finally entered the war in 1917, Alvo was interned in a Salt Lake City camp for enemy aliens. After the war he resumed his business activities in Seattle, and in 1939 became a U.S. citizen. In 1963 he died at the age of eighty-six in Seattle.

But what really happened to Bodo von Alvensleben, the brother who lived very briefly on Arcadia Street in Esquimalt? Did he leave Victoria in a hurry at the outbreak of war? Was he captured with top secret plans in his possession? Was he shot? Did he return to Germany and live many more years there to organize two assassination attempts in Berlin? Or were these too simply all rumours of no substance?

One thing is certain. His empire-building brother, Alvo, maintained to the end of his life that Canada was "a wonderful country" and he never lost faith in the future of British Columbia.

1010 Arcadia Street

SEA SCAPE

THE HOUSE OF AN ECCENTRIC PHILANTHROPIST

When people speak of politician and philanthropist John Dean today, they invariably mention the Saanich Peninsula park near Mount Newton that bears his name. This was his "beloved hilltop" where he was reputed to live a hermit's life in the cabin he built there for himself.

It is true that he did indeed purchase 80 virgin acres at the top of Mount Newton after he returned to Victoria in 1906 from his years of living in Rossland where he had served on council as both alderman and mayor. It is also true that in 1909 he decided to build a cabin which he called "Illahie" on the slopes of Mount Newton, and spent a great deal of time there alone, enjoying a peaceful life away from the pressures of business and politics.

Not quite so well known is the fact that in 1920 Dean also purchased a half-acre lot in Esquimalt for the sum of $1,000, and between 1920 and 1923 closely supervised the building of a house for himself at 572 Head Street which still stands today. It was a 2,600-square-foot home which Dean described as "a rambling house on top of a rock overlooking the Strait and the Olympics." This very solid home, still in excellent condition, has now been classified as a heritage house.

Throughout the years Dean earned a reputation as something of an eccentric because of his odd habits and strange philosophies. When he named his Esquimalt home, for instance, he wrote down over thirty options on pieces of paper before settling on one, which turned out to be "Sea Scape." His house also had some unusual features incorporated into it, such as a formal living room which spanned two storeys, and large windows which pivoted in the centre so that they could open fully. Dean also had pipes installed in the ceilings to circulate the fresh ocean air, and placed buzzers all around the house that would ring in the kitchen to let his servant know exactly where he was at all times.

Sea Scape soon became his official residence, but he did also spend a great deal of time on his mountain at Illahie. The mountain's vast surrounding wilderness appealed to his love of nature and the outdoors. And, although he enjoyed this seclusion, he did on occasion invite friends to join him at Illahie and music emanating from his old phonograph could often be heard echoing across the mountainside.

Although he claimed he had become disillusioned with politics, Dean continued to fight battles for the people of Esquimalt while living there because he felt they, in particular, had had a bad deal politically.

Soon after Sea Scape was completed, Dean announced that the first twenty-five children to knock on his door on New Year's Day every year would be put on his payroll. He found them all small jobs for which he gave them 25 cents a month. Anyone arriving later than January 1 was simply given $2 on his or her birthday. He also initiated the building of a playground on an empty lot farther down Head Street within sight of his house, so that he could watch the children playing there in the tree fort, the sand box, or on the swings. He

572 Head Street

was a gentle, caring man who never married or had children of his own but delighted in making life happier for local children.

A much travelled man, he also claimed that "marriage was the only thing in life. If there is any chance of being happy it is by being married with youngsters, but I was always too busy travelling."

Dean was born in Stretton, Cheshire, England, in 1850, and had apprenticed to a building firm there before moving to Toronto in 1873. Over the years he moved around a great deal, settling only briefly in places such as Galveston, Rossland and Victoria. He also travelled farther afield to New Zealand, Australia, China, Burma, India, and Alaska, as well as visiting the battlefields of France and South Africa, all the while becoming acquainted with foreign cultures. He called himself a student of life and developed many theories and philosophies. On the subject of his own longevity (he lived to age ninety-three) he once stated: "I have not smoked nor drunk intoxicating liquor for thirty-three years and have always walked a great deal." He also believed in hard work, watching his diet, and ignoring all meat. He was a vegetarian for most of his life.

John Dean was eccentric to the end. In 1936, seven years before his death, he had his own tombstone erected in Ross Bay Cemetery with a suitable inscription and only the date of his death left blank. The granite memorial bearing the unusual inscription typifies the man and the idealist, and reads as follows:

> It's a Rotten World, Artful Politicians are its bane. Its saving grace is the artlessness of the young and the wonders of the sky.

Dean died in Vancouver on March 28, 1943, and despite his thoughts about "this rotten world," would rest content today knowing that long after his departure from it, many people, young and old alike, are still wandering over his "beloved hilltop," finding peace and solitude as they appreciate the wonders of the sky in John Dean Park.

The attractive, rambling old house on Head Street in Esquimalt, situated on the rocky outcrop overlooking the strait and the Olympics, is a fitting memorial to a man who was just a little different from the rest.

Gorge Area

Once a lifeline to Fort Victoria from Kenneth McKenzie's Craigflower Farm, the waterway known as the Gorge Arm has had a long and varied history intrinsically tied to that of Victoria. When James Douglas first explored this inland waterway in 1843, he referred to it in his journal as the Canal of Camosack, "a narrow canal which passes the Fort and runs five miles [seven kilometres] into the interior of the island, affording at one point a water power of incalculable force, and there is an abundance of pine, with other valuable timber on its banks." Craigflower Farm ran as a most successful undertaking providing the fort with necessary food supplies and even a school, which opened in March of 1855.

Before long, the Gorge was also known for its great beauty and became a delightful retreat for boating, regattas and picnics, especially those associated with Queen Victoria's birthday celebrations on the May 24 weekend every year. Inevitably, as the years passed, many elegant homes belonging to the rich and famous also began to line the banks of the waterway, and garden parties were the height of fashion among such notables as the Grants, the Tyrwhitt-Drakes, the O'Reillys, the Dunsmuirs and the Fawcetts.

In the early part of the twentieth century, many more homes were built along Gorge Road West on the Saanich border, and some of these in the 500 to 700 blocks are still familiar landmarks today. In this section, the stories of two houses are told. One is a prominent landmark structure on Gorge Road West and the other an outstanding house situated on the tree-lined avenue known as Colquitz which stretches from Admirals Road down towards the waterway.

Although life along the Gorge Arm had changed considerably by the outbreak of the Second World War and many of the once-stately shoreline homes had disappeared, the three municipalities responsible for the Gorge (Victoria, Saanich and Esquimalt) once again began to take an active interest in the area. Improvements in the form of parks, landscaped areas, and attractive walkways slowly began to appear. Even the wildlife returned. Now, in the twenty-first century, it can finally be said that the Gorge's natural beauty and usefulness has once again been realized to its full potential.

THE LAURELS

A PROMINENT GORGE ROAD LANDMARK

Looking across the Gorge waterway, there is one particularly striking house on Gorge Road West. Its attractive pink facade, balconies, balustrades and columns help it stand out from the rest. This structure certainly piques the curiosity of anyone who is intrigued by old homes, and is reminiscent of the once-popular British India style. It is similar in design to the Dr. Charles Newcombe house at 138 Dallas Road.

The house in question is known as "The Laurels," and was built in 1913 for James M. Kellie, a retired quartz miner from the interior of B.C. He and his wife, Margaret, moved to Victoria and purchased acreage along the Gorge which had once been owned by John Lemon, one of the first Gorge landowners.

Kellie was born in Coburg, Ontario, in 1843, and as a young man had mined in the Kootenay area. In 1890 he founded the Miners' Association and involved himself in disputes between government and miners over the mining regulations of the day. It was said that when Premier John Robson visited Revelstoke on a campaign tour, Kellie (fondly known as "Pot Hole Kellie") and some of his miner friends undertook to "kidnap" the premier. In fact, they simply drove him around town airing their grievances before releasing him. The strategy worked and Robson was so impressed by Kellie's determination that he agreed to allow him to draft a new mining act which gave miners more say in how things were to be done.

This experience caused Kellie to become interested in politics, and in 1894 and 1898, he entered the political race and won the seat for the West Kootenays in the legislature. The following year he retired and went into business for himself.

Kellie married Margaret Adela Smith in 1910 and three years later the couple moved to Victoria. They soon built The Laurels which then overlooked not only the Gorge waterway but also the B.C. Electric (or Tramway) Park, and the Japanese Gardens. James Kellie died in 1927 and his widow lived on at the house until the 1930s. She died at the age of eighty-four in 1949.

Subsequent owners of The Laurels were the Davenports, the Claytons, the Redgraves, and the Days. Then, in the 1950s, a man named Gunnar Christensen purchased the elegant house and made it his life's work to keep a complete and accurate record of the house's history from 1913, including information on all the owners and/or renters who had lived there and all additions and alterations that had taken place. These meticulous records are still stored in the attic by the current owners, Ray and Linda Lee Brougham and Bob and Anne Hughes, who bought the house in July of 1999.

At the time Christensen purchased the house, he also owned the house next door (number 500), where he and his wife lived until the 1960s. During those years, they rented The Laurels to tenants while converting the house to multi-family use.

In the 1970s, Christensen decided to change the structure back to a single-family dwelling for himself, but added two suites in the basement which still remain. The current owners are very impressed with Christensen's immaculate work throughout, which has served to give the house both space and warmth. After they moved in, only minimal cosmetic painting and refinishing of floors was necessary.

The elaborate fireplace in the kitchen was imported from Finland; the stained glass in the windows and in the front door was taken from number 500; and the master bedroom fireplace, installed in 1985, has a mantel and surround made of redwood from San Francisco, with an insert from another heritage house on Linden Avenue. The fireplace in the attic came from 1602 Bank Street, and was built between 1906 and 1909. The exterior wrought-iron fire escapes surrounding the house, which were all installed in 1987, came from the Beverly Hotel on Yates Street, *circa* 1912.

Gunnar Christensen died in the house he had loved and cherished, and was greatly missed in the neighbourhood. Those who knew him remember him as a small, extremely shy man, standing barely five feet in height. He liked to take walks around the neighbourhood and, on one such walk, was invited in for tea by a neighbour. Christensen was drawn out of his shyness and enjoyed himself so much that he came up with the idea of making tea parties a regular feature among his neighbours along the Gorge waterway.

Christensen also had a Christmas routine which soon became a tradition in the neighbourhood. Every December he placed three candles on his front veranda to signify the beginning of the season. The first year without candles caused some long-time residents in the area to mention to the new owners that they missed seeing them. They had always known that once the candles appeared, the Christmas season had officially begun along the Gorge waterway. The new owners, who have taken a keen interest in their home and are proud of its heritage designation from the Saanich municipality, may decide to continue this charming tradition.

It is to be hoped that this imposing structure will long be preserved for others to enjoy from across the waters of the Gorge.

516 Gorge Road West

KOBLE HURST

THE HOUSE OF GOATS AND HORTICULTURAL DELIGHTS

One of the Gorge area's best examples of the traditional craftsman bungalow can be found on Colquitz Avenue at number 2895, the house known as "Koble Hurst."

This house was believed to have been built and designed by David H. Bale in 1911 for Cowper William Newbury on one of the four lots that Newbury had purchased from his brother John. A year earlier John Newbury had acquired twenty acres of land in the North Gorge area which originally formed part of the Thomas Porter farm. He then proceeded to subdivide the land into lots and also gave names to two streets in the area (Newbury and Cowper) to honour his parents, William and Jane (Cowper) Newbury.

William and Jane had arrived in Victoria in 1863 by way of the Panama Canal, and William soon went to work as a saddler and harness maker in a shop he bought on Yates Street. Their son John was the first British Columbia recipient of the Governor General's Medal when he graduated from Victoria High School at age fourteen. Then, in 1878, John became a teacher at Craigflower School and remained there in that capacity for five years, during which time his parents, his brother Cowper, and his four sisters lived with him in the schoolhouse teacher's accommodation. After John left the school, he went into the customs service and was collector of customs for Victoria from 1904 until he retired in 1922.

When brother Cowper purchased four of John's lots on Colquitz Avenue, he did so with the intention of building a home there and retiring to "the country." For more than twenty years he worked at the Victoria Post Office but, due to ill health in 1908, was forced to retire early at the age of forty-two. Prior to moving to Colquitz Avenue, he lived on South Turner Street in James Bay behind his parents' house on Government Street. Both of these Newbury houses have now been designated as heritage by the City of Victoria.

After Cowper Newbury and his wife Willemetta moved into Koble Hurst, they developed a large garden and began growing sweet peas and dahlias. These were displayed at many horticultural shows throughout the area, and over the years won numerous prizes.

Another hobby of Newbury's was breeding goats and he soon owned a prize-winning herd of Saanens and became a member of the B.C. Goatbreeders Association. Newbury died in 1930. His wife lived on at Koble Hurst until her death in 1972.

There are many other fine homes along this pleasant, tree-lined avenue stretching from Admirals Road down towards the Gorge waterway, and most were built after the turn of the twentieth century.

In 1912, Malcolm Houghton, a local builder, purchased several more of John Newbury's lots and built the house at 2850 Colquitz, another craftsman bungalow with a large gable over the front veranda. From 1915 until 1932, this house was owned and lived in by blacksmith Herbert Pope and his wife Laura.

2895 Colquitz Avenue

Two years later in 1914, 2833 Colquitz Avenue was built for a farmer, Charles Eaket, and his wife Agnes. Although supposedly retired, Charles still kept one cow and sold milk from his property until well into the 1920s. The house remained in the Eaket family until 1979, long after Charles' death.

Colquitz Avenue seemed to be a popular retreat for retired farmers. Number 2826, an Edwardian bungalow with wide dormers on hipped roofs, was built the same year as Koble Hurst, for Hattie and Herman O'Kelly, who were farmers from Virginia.

Today, however, it is still Koble Hurst that stands out above the rest with its veranda foundation, piers, and two chimneys all built of fieldstone. The wide front veranda has a low-pitched gable roof set on posts and lintel.

The Newburys certainly made their mark in the Gorge area. Considered then to be a "country retreat," the land John Newbury owned, the house that Cowper Newbury built, and the namesake neighbourhood roads, all serve as reminders of this interesting family.

Saanich Area

Saanich is one of the oldest agricultural settlements in British Columbia. Early settlers back in the 1850s, such as John Tod in Gordon Head and the Thompsons on the Saanich Peninsula, had the daunting task of transforming virgin forest into productive farmland.

Farming soon became the main source of livelihood in the area with Saanich dairy herds and milk products becoming world famous. By the turn of the nineteenth century, the district was also renowned for its fruit and flowers.

Since incorporation in 1906, the population of Saanich has increased considerably in a municipality today described as a bedroom community that is now both urban and rural. As a result, the residences in Saanich vary greatly in style and historic importance.

The house tales included in this section offer a glimpse into the lives of sea captains, farmers, strawberry and flower growers, writers, policemen and teachers, while adding some ghostly tales, and the story of a house that moved.

An eclectic mixture indeed of grand mansions, country cottages, urban residences and farmhouses makes up the area of Saanich, the "fair land."

DODD HOUSE

DESERTERS, DOGS AND A DASH OF DANGER

Although not on its original site, Lambrick Park's "Dodd House" has the distinction of being both the oldest house in Saanich and the first to receive heritage designation from the Saanich municipality in 1979.

When built in 1859 for Captain Charles Dodd it was described as country Georgian and stood at the northeast corner of Torquay Drive and Kenmore Road in Gordon Head. It was moved to its present site in Lambrick Park in 1978 by Charles Van Veen who purchased the house, subdivided the remaining lots, and then donated the Dodd House to the Municipality of Saanich. He moved it at his own expense, receiving a preservation award from the Hallmark Society for his generosity.

But what of the years in between, and the story of the infamous Captain Dodd himself? A Hudson's Bay Company man, he arrived in the Pacific Northwest in 1833 as second mate aboard the *Nereide*. Within two years he was an officer aboard the *Beaver*, the first steamship to operate in these waters. From 1845 until 1851 he was captain of the *Beaver*, but a temporary disagreement with members of his crew caused him to resign. He later resumed his position as captain and served until 1858.

Dodd's daring adventures during those years were legion, one of his most famous being the Christmas Hill murders when James Douglas joined Dodd to search up-island for the murderers of a shepherd on a farm at Christmas Hill. The criminals were tracked down in Nanaimo, a jury was set up aboard the *Beaver* and a verdict of guilty was brought down.

In 1859, Dodd again made news when he went in search of the scalp of his old friend, Colonel Eby, killed two years earlier by natives in the San Juan Islands. Dodd was determined to bring back this grisly relic so that the Eby family could hold a proper burial. He finally located the scalp which the newspapers of the day described thus: "in its entirety, with the hair and ears still attached. The skin, free from fleshy matter, appears white, but slightly discoloured by smoke."

In 1842 Dodd had married Grace McTavish and the couple had seven children. As a family of some importance in Victoria, the Dodds first lived in a fifteen-room mansion on ten lots bounded by Cormorant, Fisgard, and Douglas streets. At the same time, Dodd also purchased land in Gordon Head plus a 500-acre farm in the Strawberry Vale area.

Grace Dodd was the daughter of trader J.G. McTavish; a country girl at heart from her pioneering childhood years, she now desperately wanted a home of her own in the country. She eventually persuaded her husband to build a country retreat on their Gordon Head acreage. Meanwhile, Grace was causing a stir in town because of the large number of noisy dogs she owned that were frequently attacking passers-by. Neighbours were always complaining about her and being in the centre of such controversy did not please Grace who yearned for the simple country life.

Dodd House

The house the Dodds eventually built in Gordon Head was very plain in design with wooden exterior and redwood panelling interior. At the time they were one of only fourteen landowners in the area.

Unfortunately Charles Dodd did not live long enough to enjoy their country home. Soon after his promotion to chief factor, he became sick at Fort Simpson and was brought back to Victoria aboard the *Labouchere*. He died on June 2, 1860, at age fifty-one.

Three years later Grace was making news yet again. In August of 1863, she was charged with "harboring and secreting five deserters" from the British barque *Haversham* in her Gordon Head home. At that time the forests of Gordon Head were notorious for hiding law-breaking fugitives. Charles Dodd had left his large estate in the care and administration of Dr. William Fraser Tolmie and Roderick Finlayson who had taken it upon themselves to also watch over his widow, so they arranged for John Work to appear before Magistrate Pemberton and speak on Grace's behalf. As a result, a somewhat merciful court believed that Mrs. Dodd was completely unaware that she was breaking the law and merely fined her $10. By 1883, the large Dodd estate was divided up among Dodd descendants.

Subsequent owners of the Dodd House were the Pollock family who occupied the house for fifty years, Dr. John Ash, and then Captain Henry Mellin and his family. Mellin's son Andrew was married to Samuel Maclure's daughter Barbara. Mellin sold the house to Louis Worrell who renovated it during the 1960s, and the Larter family then lived there until 1978 when Charles Van Veen purchased the house and had it moved to its present location.

Today, the Dodd House belongs to the people of Saanich as a designated historical building. One renter, Nancy Griffin, who lived there from 1983 until 2000, maintained this little gem in Lambrick Park in an admirable fashion and allowed the public to view at pre-arranged times. She was also a founding member of the Dodd Society, now disbanded, which for many years preserved the memory of the colourful Captain Dodd.

Meanwhile, Captain Charles Dodd rests peacefully in Pioneer Square in the city and his little country retreat is managed and preserved by the Saanich Heritage Foundation.

4423 TYNDALL AVENUE

THE HOUSE THAT GEOFF BUILT

As the result of an exceptionally good apple crop in 1921, fruit farmer Geoffrey Vantreight, senior (often fondly referred to as "The Strawberry King of Gordon Head") decided to build a larger house for his growing family.

Geoff was the oldest son of pioneer John Vantreight who had arrived in 1884 from Ireland and established his family in a Gordon Head wilderness home. Since John's premature death in 1896, Geoff had acted as head of the family and had soon turned a considerable profit from the land his father originally purchased. In 1914, Geoff married Maud Bartholomew, daughter of John Bartholomew, a well-known antiquarian and auctioneer in Victoria. The young couple first lived in a small house on Tyndall Avenue which Geoff and his brother Sydney built together.

Geoff was often reluctant to spend money unless it was absolutely necessary but things were going exceptionally well for him by the 1920s and his good apple crop convinced him it was time to build a larger house more suitable for his family's needs.

All the lumber for his planned new "Big House" was supplied by the Cameron Lumber Company at $10.80 a thousand board feet delivered to the site. It was brought in by a team of horses that hauled it up the Tyndall hill to its final destination. The stonework on the house, which was rough-cut granite and included the veranda columns and porte-cochere, was crafted by local stonemason George Watson who was at the time reeve of Saanich, and in 1911 had built the house known as "Thrums" on Barrie Road.

When the stonework job was completed, Watson had no more work for his men, so he made Vantreight an offer. For $500 he would build a stone wall in front of the house. Vantreight agreed and, with the aid of a team of horses, hauled the good quality white granite from his own twenty-seven acres for Watson and his men to cut, enabling them to erect the wall which still stands today.

A hexagonal cupola was built on top of the house from which a 360-degree panoramic view could be enjoyed. Geoff used it as a lookout across the surrounding countryside. Bay windows on two sides of the house and arches on the porte-cochere and porch were added. The porte-cochere was then topped by a wooden-railed balcony. Other balconies are located on the south and east sides of the house, encompassing a conservatory.

The walls of the house were stuccoed and the gables half-timbered. The windows are a mixture of both horizontal and arched design, emphasizing an eclectic style of Geoff Vantreight's creation. In 1922, the house was ready for occupancy.

Down through the decades, memories abound concerning the Big House. Geoff senior's children recall growing up there. A wedding reception for one daughter was held there, and a son, Geoff junior, met his future wife, Jean, for the first time under the porte-cochere when she arrived with a group of his friends for an evening out. Geoff senior also raised chinchillas in the basement of the Big House at one time.

Those who worked summer jobs at the Vantreight Farms back in the 1950s also recall the familiar sight of Geoff senior on the porch of his house, dressed in his Stanfield underwear with braces holding up well-worn pants, his tattered fedora with air vents cut into the crown covering his head. Invariably he would be shouting instructions across the yard to his namesake son or to his workers.

Numerous grandchildren later played in the grounds of the Big House. Its circular driveway was ideal for go-kart racing, a popular family pastime, and neighbourhood Halloween parties were an annual event at the Vantreights.

Although the house is still family owned, it is now rented to tenants. There is a certain irony in the fact that one tenant practiced the ancient art of bookbinding in the basement of the Big House. Geoff Vantreight, senior, who died in 1959, was a man who always admired old-fashioned methods, and would have approved of a business which dates back centuries to a tradition that initially began as a way to protect parchment manuscripts. In today's world, bookbinding is often still done by hand.

Knowing that such an ancient craft had been practiced in the house he built with love and pride so long ago would most definitely have pleased the Strawberry King of Gordon Head.

4423 Tyndall Avenue

4320 TORQUAY DRIVE

THE GRANTS OF GORDON HEAD

The house which today stands at 4320 Torquay Drive is the last of the three houses in the Gordon Head area which once belonged to the Grants, a prominent pioneer family in the area.

Brothers William and James Grant arrived in Canada from Scotland in 1883 and worked their way west by finding employment on the Canadian Pacific railway line. The two brothers were also witness to the historic driving of the last spike at Craigellachie. When they eventually reached Victoria, William found work at Craigdarroch Castle, using his talents on the interior woodwork, and James embarked on a career in the city, eventually becoming British Columbia's markets commissioner.

William and his wife Bella lived in a house on Wark Street, but they also purchased land in the area of today's Tyndall Avenue in Gordon Head from Dr. John Ash. The first home they built on this acreage was named "Homewood" and they soon moved there with their son, Charlie. In 1891 a second son, James, was born and that same year, William Grant, along with John Vantreight and William Dean, was instrumental in getting the first school built in Gordon Head: Gordon Head Elementary.

The Grants lived at Homewood for nine years during which time four more children were born to them. It was a hard pioneering life with long treks into town for supplies and the constant necessity of keeping the land clear and preventing wildlife from destroying their crops.

The Grants soon saw that there was money to be made in strawberry farming so they successfully embarked upon that enterprise. William donated some of his Tyndall Avenue land for the building of a community hall, known as the Gordon Head Mutual Improvement Society Hall, at the top of Tyndall Hill. This hall was later moved to its present location on Tyndall at the rear of Lambrick Park. William was one of the first trustees of the society and contributed over thirty years of his life to serving the community.

Soon after donating the land for the community hall, the Grants moved to their second home which they named "Craigellachie." This house was later renamed "Strangewood" and burned to the ground many years later. There is a house called Strangewood today on the same site.

While living at Craigellachie, the Grants continued to prosper with their strawberry-growing enterprise, but Bella Grant still insisted on making her own soap, vinegar, dried prunes and apple rings. She also found time to indulge in a monthly "at home" day with other pioneer women in the neighbourhood where they would reminisce together about the "old country."

Soon after the turn of the nineteenth century, Grant purchased part of the Pollock land, originally part of the Dodd estate, and there they built their third and last home which today is 4320 Torquay Drive. The Grants even had the house wired for electricity, anticipating things to come, but ironically, by the time lines were installed in Gordon Head by the British

4320 Torquay Drive

Columbia Electric Company, the Grants had left the district to retire in the Cariboo.

The historical importance of 4320 Torquay Drive, therefore, lies primarily in the fact that it is the only one still standing of the three Grant houses once located in Gordon Head. After they sold it and through the years, much of the original fabric of the house was altered. The old porch was framed in and used as an additional bedroom. Consequently, the appearance of the house from the front changed considerably. Steep stairs with wrought-iron railings were added, and all but one of the original windows were replaced with modern ones. Two leaded-glass windows were added beside the fireplace.

By 1995, ceilings were cracked and sagging badly. French doors had replaced the original dining-room bay windows, and a totally-out-of-character sundeck had been added to the front upstairs bedroom. In addition, the duroid roof was leaking and in need of repair.

Such was the state of the Grant house when new owners John Clemens and Patricia Ball presented the Saanich Heritage Foundation with a three-phase restoration plan for the 1905 heritage residence.

Phase one undertook the restoration of the porch and front entrance, upper deck on the front, the south side deck, and the replacement of stained-glass windows plus hardware for the front door. Phase two involved replacing the remaining windows and restoring the rear deck. Phase three kicked in in 1997 and meant re-roofing with cedar shingles and painting the exterior in modified colours of pale green, cream, and red-brown.

All the interior work was undertaken by John and Pat themselves, with the help and guidance of a master carpenter, David Helland, and it was estimated by the owners that they spent well over 4,000 hours stripping woodwork and performing other chores. During the whole operation, "before and after" photographs were taken by John and Pat who, being totally dedicated to authenticity, had thoroughly researched the history of the house and all its past owners. Their goal was to reflect the style and times of the original structure built by the Grant family.

The end result justifiably earned them a heritage preservation award from the Hallmark Society in 1998. Today, 4320 Torquay Drive is an admirable monument to one of Gordon Head's most notable pioneer strawberry farming families.

1861 FERNDALE ROAD

DOWN A LEAFY LANE IN GORDON HEAD

Tucked way back from the road down a long, leafy lane in Gordon Head stands a house which would probably go unnoticed by most people. However, its interesting history and especially one of its very well-known past owners, make 1861 Ferndale Road more than worthy of a closer look.

According to Judith Terry, the house's present owner, who is a University of Victoria professor and novelist, the house has always been a warm, happy home where "good things happen," and its long and varied history since 1914 certainly bears this out.

It was originally built (and believed to have been designed) by Saanich builder, Edward James Merritt, for John Fullerton, a second engineer from 1877 to 1878 on the *Beaver*. Until his death in 1939, Fullerton was the last surviving officer of that famous ship. When he retired to Gordon Head at age sixty, 1861 Ferndale Road became his home. He then decided to try his hand at strawberry farming.

Following Fullerton, the house was acquired by Lieutenant-Colonel the Reverend A. Woods, a padre in the First World War, and his wife Henrietta. They took over ownership in 1920 and, in order to supplement his pension, Woods began to grow tulips on his property for commercial purposes, but pretty soon he had some strong competition in the neighbourhood. He also had an orchard of 150 cherry trees.

By far the best-known owner of the house, however, was writer Nellie McClung. She and her husband Wesley moved there in 1935. At that time, most people in the neighbourhood were unaware of this lady's significant contributions to social reform. Teacher and author, Nellie McClung was born in Ontario in 1873, and by 1908 had written the first of her many books, *Sowing Seeds in Danny*, destined to become a best seller.

Long before she moved to Gordon Head, McClung had been active in many areas. She was the only woman to attend the Canadian War Conference in 1918, and the first woman to attend the World Ecumenical Conference in 1921. She had been a Liberal member of the Alberta legislature from 1921 until 1926, and in 1928 was one of the "famous five" Alberta women who had attempted to have women declared "persons"in the nationally famous "Persons Case."

Controversial and free-thinking, McClung became the first woman to serve on the board of governors of the CBC, and the first woman elder in the United Church of Canada, as well as the only woman included in the delegation to the League of Nations.

Despite her hectic life as a crusader for women's rights, she also raised five children and was a prolific writer of everything from essays to novels. During the time she lived in the Ferndale Road house, 1935 to 1951, she gave her house the name "Lantern Lane" because of the lantern she always kept hanging at the end of the lane. While living there, she penned two books, *Leaves from Lantern Lane,* and the second volume of her autobiography, *The Streams*

Run Fast. A converted coach house behind the home became McClung's study and it was there that she apparently wrote her works.

In 1973, long after her death, a stamp was issued to honour the hundredth anniversary of Nellie McClung's birth, and the people of Gordon Head at last fully realized the significant impact their well-loved neighbour had had upon society. Today, a library at the corner of McKenzie Avenue and Cedar Hill Road bears her name.

There have been only three other owners of the Ferndale house since the McClungs: the Dabinetts who were involved in market gardening; the Tregears in real estate; and, since 1981, Reginald and Judith Terry have been in residence.

The current owners especially enjoy the peace and seclusion of their home which Judith Terry describes as "a comfortable home with a lovely, pleasant design." Its atmosphere, she says, is "perfect" and probably conducive to yet another author living under its roof.

Even today, an occasional visitor will still wander up the lane to reminisce with the owners about Nellie McClung and the years she spent as part of the neighbourhood while living in the intriguing, old house down that leafy lane in Saanich.

1861 Ferndale Road

THRUMS

THE HOUSE WITH A LITERARY CONNECTION

When Sir James M. Barrie, best known for his classic *Peter Pan,* wrote the book *A Window in Thrums* in 1889, he little realized that a house built thousands of miles away in Canada would one day be named in honour of his work.

The book, set in Barrie's native village of Kirriemuir, Scotland, describes a special window in the house known as "Thrums" as "the square foot of glass where Jess sat in her chair and looked down the brae." And today, at the front of Thrums on Barrie Road in Gordon Head, high up under the peak of the roof, there is a small, special window similar to the one in Barrie's book.

The explanation for this literary connection is simple. James Barrie had a young cousin named George Watson who emigrated from Scotland to Canada when he was seventeen; Watson was the man who later built Thrums and named it to commemorate his famous cousin.

Before heading west, Watson had spent time in Ontario. Once he arrived on the west coast, he established himself as a stonemason of note in Victoria. An interest in music and choral work, where his tenor voice was put to good use in the choirs of Calvary Baptist and the First Presbyterian churches, eventually led Watson to meet Elizabeth Grant. (It happened to be the first Sunday after she arrived in Victoria to join her two brothers, William and James Grant.) George Watson and Elizabeth Grant were soon married and, in 1903, the young couple moved to Gordon Head.

They first purchased "Jersey Hall" from Dr. John Ash, after whom Ash Road is named and who served as provincial secretary from 1872 to 1874. Dr. Ash had chosen the name Jersey Hall in memory of his father-in-law, Sir John Veuille, high sheriff of Jersey in the Channel Islands.

Later, the Watsons decided they wanted to build a home of stone, the material with which George Watson loved to work and was more familiar. Thrums was the result. The interior wood panelling of the house was the work of a pioneer carpenter, Isaac Sommers. Finally completed in 1911, the four-bedroom house ideally suited the Watsons and their three daughters.

George Watson was a familiar sight riding to town on his bicycle. He worked on such buildings as the Carnegie Library on Yates Street, the old post office building, and the Gisburn estate wall on Rockland Avenue. Years later, the stone dust began to affect his health so he turned his attention to farming. Watson's cherries and strawberries became famous in the area.

George Watson also ran twice for reeve of Saanich and, as the area of Gordon Head was still without piped water in 1920, his campaign slogan became "Watson and Water." He eventually died in 1930 at the age of sixty-two.

His wife, Elizabeth, was long remembered for her community work, both with the Red Cross and the Gordon Head Women's Institute formed in 1914.

1775 Barrie Road

She was the first president of the latter organization. She also ran the Gordon Head post office for fourteen years in the small, glass-walled room by the back door of Thrums, until it closed down in 1920. One of the Watsons' daughters, Marjorie Goodwin, became a teacher at the original Gordon Head Elementary School.

Today, newer homes encroach upon the area that once surrounded Thrums, an area which was the habitat for deer, cougars and even bears. But despite the property's diminished size, Thrums itself remains a well-preserved heritage home and, best of all, is still family owned and occupied today by George Watson's grandson.

1542 MOUNT DOUGLAS CROSS ROAD

A GHOST AT THE CROSS ROADS?

Mount Douglas Cross Road is a long, winding road, curving its way from Cedar Hill Road into the Blenkinsop Valley. It did not, however, always bear the name of the little mountain nearby. The road was once known as Glendenning Road after Adam Glendinning, an early settler in the Blenkinsop Valley, and in those days it wound its way to the foot of the mountain trail.

There are a number of houses of note along this winding road, but none with a more interesting history than the house that stands at number 1542. It was built in 1912 for Kate and Arthur Meacock, fruit growers who had previously resided on Tyndall Avenue, but records show that the Meacocks only lived on Mount Douglas Cross Road for approximately two years.

By the 1920s, a pheasant farm was being operated on the property – many oldtimers in the neighbourhood still remember those days. For years after the pheasant farmer had left, the occasional pheasant could still be seen roaming the area.

An owner who lived at 1542 during the 1950s and 1960s recalls that when doing renovations, he discovered numerous pairs of old riding boots that had been discarded in the crawl space and had become home for an army of mice. He suspects that at some point a riding school might also have operated from the property. And when ripping out walls, he found newspapers dating back to the turn of the century. There were also at least four layers of baseboard in some areas of the house.

More recent owners have discovered another wrinkle in the history of this house, namely some friendly ghosts. Being sensible, down-to-earth folk, not given to fanciful notions, they have naturally found it difficult to accept the existence of ghosts in their home. However, at various times over the years, they have been aware of a strange presence in their midst.

A ghost first appeared in the form of shadows moving down the hallway towards the dining room. A medium who once visited the house confirmed that these impressions are strongest in the area of the dining room where reflections of a man wearing a tweed jacket have been seen in a mirror. One visitor to the house dropped his coffee cup in alarm because he felt the ghost's presence so strongly.

An incident which may have taken place in the 1920s or early 1930s could explain these apparitions. The people living there at that time were well-to-do folk who entertained guests from around the world on a grand scale with many banquets and garden parties. The story goes that one gentleman visitor from Germany by the name of Karl fell in love with the young lady of the house, but his attentions were not reciprocated and she adamantly rejected him. In desperation he hanged himself in the attic.

The tragedy of this unrequited love is supposedly the reason that Karl continues to return to the house on the cross roads, manifesting himself in ghostly form, to search for his lost love, Marilyn, who has also been seen on occasion.

The story of this sad love affair may or may not be true, but the owners of the house, and visitors to it through the years, all believe there is definitely something odd going on within its walls. As the ghostly visits are invariably warm and friendly, they have now become an accepted way of life for the occupants of number 1542.

As though to confirm their beliefs, the owners later also learned that one corner of their house stands directly on a native Indian spiritual burial path which runs along Mount Douglas Cross Road – a fact which might also account for some of these ghostly encounters.

As an added, somewhat amusing, piece of information about this house, some of the bathroom fixtures originally came from the bishop's palace on View Street in Victoria. Today, the present owner states she feels "very holy" when taking a bath, knowing she is sitting where the bishop once sat!

1542 Mount Douglas Cross Road

1279 TATTERSALL DRIVE

THE CHRISTMAS HOUSE WITH A CRIDGE CONNECTION

Where is there a house in Greater Victoria that in its lifetime has had two front doors, two house numbers, a past occupant who was a well-known portrait artist, one current owner who is a descendant of the famous Bishop Cridge, and another with a possible connection to Scottish novelist Sir Walter Scott?

If all that is not enough to intrigue and tantalize, this particular house also has a strong tie to the Christmas season. As one of the houses at the top end of Tattersall Drive, for many years it formed part of the annual "Candy Cane Lane" extravaganza which celebrated its final year in 1999.

Number 1279 Tattersall Drive sits majestically on a rock formation and is believed to have been built in the mid-1930s for a Mr. Nordal. In 1946, the house, which at that time was numbered 1275, was traded by Nordal for property on Goldstream Avenue. The lady who traded her acreage was Hester Wilkinson, a portrait artist of note who for many years had a photography studio on the second floor of the Stobart Building on Yates Street. She purchased the studio in 1931 from Edwin Easthope and through the years painted many of Victoria's leading citizens including Archbishop Sexton and Lieutenant-Governor Eric Hamber. Ironically, the current owner, Rob Laundy, discovered that his own father had also had his portrait painted by Hester in her Yates Street studio back in the 1930s.

Soon after she moved into the house, Hester Wilkinson's health deteriorated and she decided to relocate her studio from downtown to her home on Tattersall Drive. For this, she had the in-house garage enlarged and the electrical service upgraded to accommodate the special lighting which was needed.

In those days the property was much larger than it is today. The west side of the house had a ramped concrete driveway leading into the basement studio and a flight of stairs wound up to the front door. There was also a sunken garden on the side that today is occupied by an adjoining house.

Hester sold the house in 1960 and for the next thirty years there were approximately a dozen owners. Subdividing of the property took place in 1976 and many alterations were made to 1275, including moving the front door to the east side and giving the house a new number, 1279. In addition, decks were added off the den and the dining room.

Gerri and Rob Laundy purchased the house in the early 1990s and one of the happiest events to take place there was their wedding in 1992. Gerri said she immediately loved "the diversity and space of the home for a blended family." Her teen-aged children enjoyed their large attic bedrooms and the enormous recreation room on the main floor which enabled them to entertain their friends, while Rob and Gerri had their own private den upstairs.

Through the years since, the Laundys have undertaken more renovations and alterations both inside and out. In 1992 they changed the traditional black trim and white stucco to a Wedgewood blue trim and cream stucco. The interior of their home now has hardwood flooring, and they have gutted and

1279 Tattersall Drive

modernized bathrooms, as well as transforming the large recreation room into an office. French doors have added a heritage look to the home and the small kitchen has also recently undergone a major renovation. Landscaping has included more rock work with gardens and pathways, and a double garage has replaced the carport.

Like other residents of "Candy Cane Lane," the Laundys always enjoyed participating in the Christmas spectacle each year which they tried to keep simple yet effective without being glitzy. Large spotlights placed on the rocks highlighted the smaller waterfall-type lights covering the rock formation, while a huge red bow on the house and garage (initiated by Gerri's daughter, Jenny) and a star over the oak tree lighting up the dark sky were added features. Rob played Santa Claus several times and Gerri's son, Dan, also took on the role on one occasion. One year the Reynolds School Band came by to play outside the house, and a candlelit singsong was a popular addition to the festivities on another occasion.

Rob Laundy's ancestry dates back to Victoria's Bishop Cridge via his grandfather, Thomas H. Laundy, who was born in London. There he trained in law and eventually came to Victoria and met Ellen Cridge, the bishop's daughter. The couple married in 1891 and lived in a Simcoe Street house at the back of the Cridge property. Thomas Laundy worked for the Bank of Commerce and later became a minister serving at the Church of Our Lord. Rob's father, Arthur, was one of Thomas and Ellen Laundy's six children. In his spare time, Rob has been working on an extensive family tree for both the Cridge and Laundy families.

The Laundys' respective pasts do not end there. Gerri's ancestry may well be associated with the famous Scotsman, Sir Walter Scott. Her grandmother, Grace Lockhart, firmly believed their ancestors had Scott connections; one of them, J.G. Lockhart, was Scott's well-known biographer. Gerri is still trying to confirm the connection through her research.

Meanwhile, the Laundys continue to enjoy their unique home on Tattersall Drive, full of character and warmth and a collection of fascinating history within its walls.

1140 TATTERSALL DRIVE

THE SAANICH DOCTOR WHO WITNESSED THE CAPTURE OF AN INFAMOUS MURDERER

Today, 1140 Tattersall Drive, an elegant 1912 Tudor-revival mansion, and now a multi-dwelling residence, is tucked back down a long driveway well hidden behind more recent residential development. The original owner of this lovely house had an interesting connection to Marconi, the inventor of the wireless telegraph, and to the notorious British criminal, Hawley Harvey Crippen.

The house in question was designed by Harold R. Rous Cullin, a Saanich School Board architect, for Dr. Valentine de Saumerez Duke and his wife, Mary Sarah. Among Cullin's other designs is the elegant building on Boleskine Road, once Mount Tolmie School and now the home of the school board offices.

Dr. Duke had led a fascinating life before coming to Canada and retiring in Saanich. He was born in Ireland, trained as a doctor, and eventually became ship's surgeon for the Peninsular and Oriental Steamship Line. He also worked for thirty years in Ceylon where he encouraged the growth and manufacture of cinchona for quinine production.

But it was while crossing the Atlantic on his way to Canada in 1910 aboard the steamship *Montrose* that his most exciting adventure took place. Exactly one hundred and thirty miles west of Lizard Point, Cornwall, a telegraph was sent by the captain of the vessel to the police which read as follows:

> Have strong suspicions that Crippen, the London cellar murderer and accomplice are among saloon passengers...moustache taken off...growing beard...accomplice dressed as boy but voice manner and build undoubtedly a girl, both travelling as Mr and Master Robinson.

Anticipating trouble as a result of the discovery and arrest by authorities of murderer Hawley Harvey Crippen, Captain Kendall alerted Dr. Duke – the only physician on board. The captain asked the doctor to stand by in case his medical services were required. As it turned out, the arrest took place without incident and Dr. Duke was not needed, other than as an observer.

But Crippen's arrest had made history around the world, not only because of the horror of his crime, but also because this was the first time that Marconi's new invention of wireless telegraphy was put to use in order to catch a criminal.

Crippen was born in Michigan in 1862, but at the age of twenty-one had gone to England to study medicine and eventually acquired a diploma as an eye and ear specialist. He also spent a short time practicing dentistry. His second wife was a music-hall performer whose stage name was Belle Elmore. Although Belle had agreed to divorce her husband, she planned on taking all their joint savings with her when she left him. This angered her normally mild husband to the point of aggression. After poisoning her with hyoscine and placing her dismembered body in the cellar of his house in Camden Town, he made his escape with his lover, Ethel le Neve, who travelled with him in disguise as a young boy. The couple posed under the names of Mr. Robinson and son. Ethel le Neve was supposedly unaware of the crime her man had committed, but nonetheless was seen wearing the late Mrs. Crippen's jewellery.

Once the captain became suspicious of their odd behaviour, he wired Chief Inspector Dew in London who was in charge of the case. Dew immediately caught a fast steamer to Canada which overtook the slower *Montrose*. He then transferred to a pilot boat and boarded the vessel to arrest the fugitives. Ethel, unaware of any danger, had been in the middle of an Edgar Wallace crime mystery when the warrant for her arrest was executed.

In November of 1910, a jury took only twenty-seven minutes to find Crippen guilty, and he was sentenced to death by hanging. Ethel le Neve was tried separately and found not guilty as an accessory after the fact. On 23 November, Crippen was hanged at Pentonville Prison in London and, at his request, a photograph of Ethel le Neve was buried with him. Ethel herself went on to live a long, fulfilling life, dying in 1967 at the age of eighty-four.

As for Dr. Duke, he arrived safely in Canada after his exciting voyage, and eventually built the home on Tattersall Drive where he and his wife, together with their younger children, lived happily for many years.

From 1928 until 1965, the property was owned by their daughter Ruby and her husband Richard Snape. Snape designed many changes to the house when it was converted to apartments in 1952. It was named the "Avoca Apartments" by Ruby to honour the kennels where she bred prize Irish setters.

Their daughter, Alison Leamy, was one of the many owners of another heritage home, the Robert Clark House, a Gothic, Queen-Anne-style structure at the corner of Mount Douglas Cross Road and Cedar Hill Road which, like her grandfather's house on Tattersall Drive, is now surrounded by newer homes.

1140 Tattersall Drive

3301 CAMROSE COURT

A HOUSE THAT ECHOES THE CALL OF THE WILD

Described as one of Saanich's best examples of the craftsman style, 3301 Camrose Court is situated just a short distance from Cook Street. Turning up Camrose Crescent which leads into Camrose Court, one is immediately aware of the large, elegant house that dominates all others in the neighbourhood.

Set in its elevated position, it affords magnificent views of the city. It was built in 1913 for Charles and Jenette French and has an interesting connection to the days of Canada's fur trade and dog-sled travel in the far north.

Charles French was born in Markham, Ontario, in 1867, and joined the Hudson's Bay Company around 1887 in general service. From 1891 until 1894 he acted as a dog-sled driver and fisherman at Lower Fort Garry, and for the next four years spent time at Port Simpson as a "general servant." Then, after many years of trading in all parts of British Columbia, he moved to Victoria as a purchasing agent in 1902, and became district manager for British Columbia by 1914. His success with the HBC enabled him to build his grand home on Camrose Court in 1913. However, although French certainly left his mark on the Camrose Court house, he did not occupy it for long.

From 1919 until 1927, he served as district manager in Vancouver and from there he moved to Winnipeg where he became chief factor and fur trade commissioner at the Hudson's Bay Company headquarters until 1930. On December 31, 1930, he officially retired from the company and returned to Victoria to live in a house on Gorge Road. In addition to his Gorge Road house, French also owned a summer cottage, called "Idletryste," at Cordova Bay.

Like his contemporary, Herbert H. Hall (another "giant" in the north who had joined the HBC in 1896), French was often called upon in retirement to relate stories of his early adventures as a fur trader in the north. As there were many interesting tales to tell, he was constantly in demand as a speaker.

Herbert Hall also had Victoria connections. He was educated here and made many lifelong friends, including one-time Victoria mayor, Bert Todd (owner of 721 Linden Avenue). Like French, Hall had served the company in many capacities ranging from purser aboard the S.S. *Saskatchewan* to dog-sledder and trader in some of the most remote areas of Canada's north.

Both men could relate hair-raising tales of learning how to build adequate shelter in sub-zero temperatures, how to survive on venison and fish, and simply how to endure extreme temperature conditions. Full of good humour about their adventures, company men often dismissed the exaggerated reports of wolf attacks, maintaining that during many thousands of miles of dog-team treks they were never bothered by the animals. French and Hall could also both speak with authority on any number of subjects from the establishment of the police force in the north to early murders which often went unsolved.

While Charles French and his wife were enjoying a well-earned retirement in Victoria in the 1930s, Hall was still operating as an independent trader in

3301 Camrose Court

the north, having broken his ties with the HBC in 1924. Hall died on the job in May 1938, doing what he enjoyed doing most, dog-sledding across the frozen waste some fifty miles from the nearest trading post.

Charles and Jenette had five children, one of whom, Leonard French, also worked for the HBC. Leonard was born in Victoria in August of 1907 and by the 1920s was working as an apprentice in the fur room of the HBC Vancouver district office. By 1946 he was acting as manager at Prince Albert and in June of that year, he resigned from the company but remained in the fur business, being first connected with Little Bros. in Vancouver, and by 1957 working for the Seattle Fur Exchange. Charles Hunt French died in September of 1940, long after he had vacated his home on Camrose Court. The house, however, could most probably still tell many exciting tales of the lives and times of those adventurous Hudson's Bay Company men.

There have been numerous other owners of the house since the 1920s when Charles French and his family gave up occupancy. Other names down the years have included Theodore and Mary Miles, Sarah and Ralph Snider, John and Eva Yeats, Andrew and June Yeats, the Oak Crest Construction Company Ltd., and Richard Richmond. Since 1983, however, the French house has been owned and enjoyed by Victoria bookstore owner, Mel Bolen.

1911 WOODLEY ROAD

A MACLURE MASTERPIECE

At the turn of the twentieth century, the area surrounding Mount Tolmie was mostly rural and there were few houses cluttering the attractive countryside. A few years later, houses began to appear at regular intervals, one even on the slopes of the mountain itself. Built in 1908 for Thory and May Thorburn, it was named "Thordis" and still stands today at 1915 Mayfair Drive.

There were soon many other houses of note on Ernest Avenue and Woodley and Waterloo roads, leading off Richmond Avenue. One of particular note is the immaculate Tudor-revival Samuel Maclure house at 1911 Woodley Road.

The house was built in 1913-14 for Maggie Susannah and Charles Bentley Jones at a cost of $4,000. Jones was a civil engineer and contractor by profession, a partner in the firm of Jones and Rant Limited, a company which began as fence builders and expanded to include roads, waterworks, drainage and construction in general. The original roof of the Woodley Road house was covered with cedar and rubber tiles by the Sidney Rubber Roofing Company (with whom Jones had business connections), but within a few years it was leaking badly and the house had to be re-roofed.

Jones and Norman Rant had initially been in business together during the Yukon gold-rush days. A colonial-style house near the corner of Lily Avenue and Quadra Street was built in 1937 for Norman Rant. Rant was an interesting man, born in India, who arrived in B.C. in 1897 and became a mining recorder in the Yukon where he met Jones. By 1899, Rant and Jones had formed a company of mining brokers and notaries public in Atlin, B.C.

While Jones became interested in civic affairs and politics, Rant was acting as proprietor of the once-famous Angela Hotel on Burdett Avenue by 1908. The Angela had originally been a prestigious girls' school known as Angela College in honour of the benevolent baroness, Angela Burdett Coutts, a banking heiress who invested a great deal of money in charitable organizations in Victoria.

Jones meanwhile served for many years as a Saanich school trustee and councillor, and, in 1919, was elected reeve of Saanich. He left Victoria with his family in 1921 for what was intended to be an extended trip touring New Zealand. Jones discovered, however, when he returned to Victoria, that the city was in an economic slump and his partner, Rant, had disappeared. Almost broke, he returned to New Zealand in 1922 to make a living there. For a while the Woodley Road house was rented to a Mr. Eakins.

Then, in 1924, 1911 Woodley Road was sold to Arthur Wilby and ten years later another sale placed the house in the hands of the Pope family. Edgar William Pope, a French Canadian, was the commanding officer at Work Point Barracks. His father had been secretary to Sir John A. Macdonald. The next owner was the Considine family and in the late 1960s the original shingle siding was stuccoed over.

In 1977, this beautiful home was purchased by Sheila and James Colwill who have undertaken extensive restoration work both inside and out. All the interior woodwork, which had been painted, was stripped; outside the stucco was removed and new window surrounds built. The newly restored garage, faced in stone, was designed by James Colwill. As it was a designated heritage house, the Colwills were assisted on part of the exterior restoration work with grants from the Saanich Heritage Foundation, and in 1989, received the Hallmark Society's Award of Merit for their work.

The Colwills, who have lived at 1911 for twenty-five years, think that most of the past owners must feel the same way about the house as they do. They have been contacted by many of them and, in particular, descendants of the Jones family (the original owners) have become regular correspondents and have passed on many interesting anecdotes.

They have learnt, for instance, that Grandfather Samuel Foulkes Jones at one time lived above the old garage where he was taken care of by a retired sailor. Despite Prohibition, this man managed to acquire frequent supplies of liquor for Mr. Jones' enjoyment. Grandfather Jones would also often wander away and become lost. A neighbour recalled that she was fascinated by him as a child because he could catch flies in his mouth – and then eat them! In addition, Charles Bentley Jones kept beehives on his property, and a cougar was apparently once spotted in the vicinity of the house.

Even though the Jones family's stay there was brief, children, grandchildren, and even great-grandchildren from New Zealand, still consider 1911 Woodley Road the old family homestead in Victoria.

It is easy to see why they would feel that way. This Maclure masterpiece is special at all times of the year, but at Christmas it takes on an almost Dickensian aura. With logs burning in the fireplace, the aroma of apple cider and cinnamon wafting from the kitchen, and greenery decorating its many delightful rooms, a visit here is like stepping back in time.

1911 Woodley Road

4366 BLENKINSOP ROAD

FROM FARMING TO BED-AND-BREAKFAST

At the turn of the twentieth century many pioneers in Victoria chose the beautiful Blenkinsop Valley to put down their roots. The valley was named for George Blenkinsop, a former employee of the Hudson's Bay Company, who purchased several hundred acres there.

One Saanich pioneer who chose the valley was William Mercer. Originally from Preston in Lancashire, England, Mercer came to Canada in 1887. By 1890, he had moved to Victoria with his wife Rebecca. Two years later their son, Robert, was born.

The Mercers' first home was on the corner of Alpha and Gamma streets from which William operated a small dairy farm. As this business grew, he moved to Burnside Road, but by 1902 had decided to purchase more extensive acreage in the Blenkinsop Valley from Adam Glendinning.

In 1909, the Mercer family moved to the valley and built their farm which they called "Lake View," being situated near what was then Lost Lake (now known as Blenkinsop Lake). Lost Lake had been so named after a British naval officer who lost his way in that area during a paper chase. The Mercer farm stood on Blenkinsop Road which in those days was also known as Lost Lake Road.

The whole area was thick with deer and occasionally farmers were woken in the night by the howling of wolves. Many of the local farmers lost their sheep to these predators. Surrounding the lake was a 600-acre swamp extending southeast towards Braefoot Road. This provided a great hunting ground for ducks, but the Mercers were more interested in their mixed farming activities. They kept sheep, turkeys and cows, both Holsteins and Jerseys.

In 1916, Robert Mercer married Gertrude Yarewood, and Robert's father gave the young couple the house which stands today at 4366 Blenkinsop Road as a wedding present. Built and designed by contractor William Drysdale, it was completed at a cost of $2,600. Robert and Gertrude had two daughters, Phyllis and Muriel.

Pioneer William Mercer died in 1925 and his son, Robert, sold off the remainder of the Mercer land in 1981 to the Mann family. For some years thereafter the house was rented. Robert Mercer died at the grand age of ninety-eight in 1988.

In 1991 the Mercer house was purchased by Ruth and Alan Holmes. For some twenty years prior to their purchase Ruth had often gazed lovingly at the house as she passed by, hoping that one day she might own it. Since they became the house's owners, many of their friends and acquaintances have told them it was also their favourite house in the neighbourhood.

During their ten years of occupancy, the Holmes have done some restoration work and basic cosmetic improvements to the home, replacing the foundation and adding dormers, as well as updating the plumbing and electricity.

One of Robert and Gertrude's two daughters, Phyllis, still lives on Blenkinsop Road in close proximity to the old Mercer family farmhouse and

4366 Blenkinsop Road

often visits with the Holmes. She recalls her parents sitting under the apple tree in the back garden enjoying their afternoon tea every day, and growing their dahlias and geraniums to the delight of the neighbourhood. On one occasion, she remembered her parents had stored a large amount of squash in the attic. The weight of it was so great that it came through the floor and landed in the middle of the kitchen.

Today the attractive Mercer home overlooking the Blenkinsop Valley is run by Ruth and Alan Holmes as a heritage bed-and-breakfast.

4201 QUADRA STREET

THE BULL HOUSE

Number 4201 Quadra, at the corner of Quadra and Beckwith streets, is an imposing structure more popularly known in the area as "the Bull house."

It was built in 1908 by dairy farmer Josiah Bull, who was born in Hilton, Huntingdonshire, in 1864, and who settled in the Victoria area specifically to begin farming here. In 1887 he married Ellen Speed, daughter of Thomas Speed, another early pioneer who had arrived in 1863 aboard the *Helvetia* to farm in the Whittier/Boleskine area of Saanich. Thomas Speed's other daughter, Rosette, married Benjamin Axhorn who worked on the sealing schooners for many years before building the house at 430 Boleskine and going to work for the British American Paint Company (BAPCO).

Josiah and Ellen Bull meanwhile had purchased forty acres of land near Elk Lake from G.W. Anderson where they started their first dairy farm. Bull also cut cordwood during this period for the Victoria Waterworks pumping stations in order to keep their boilers fueled.

The Bulls' first house on this acreage was an eight-room home at Cherry Tree Bend near where the Patricia Bay Highway runs today, but around 1907 Josiah purchased more acreage on North Quadra, moved his dairy farm business to that location, and then built the stone house which stands at 4201 Quadra Street the following year. He named it "Manor House" as a reminder of his birthplace in England. The Cherry Tree Bend house was used as a feed barn in subsequent years.

The elegant wrought-iron gates in front of Manor House were interfaced with its name, and the style of the home was Edwardian vernacular. The house was built with fieldstone by mason Alfred W. Roberts and carpenters Harry Miles and George Rudd. It is believed to be the only one in the Victoria area with ornamental mortar pointing in red, and it was also the only stone house that Alfred Roberts built.

Josiah and Ellen Bull had eleven children in all, seven girls and four boys. One of their daughters, Elizabeth, was the first stenographer to work for the municipality of Saanich. Their youngest son, Josiah junior (known as "Joe"), married a Sidney girl, Gladys Fairclough, and joined the Saanich police force on March 1, 1930. Joe had always been interested in police work, even though his early years were spent growing up on his father's farm. He still remembered as a child seeing the police dressed in khaki uniforms, patrolling on horseback, and this had appealed to his imagination.

From 1930 onwards he dedicated himself to the force, and in those early days, it was indeed a hard path to have chosen. The force at the time Joe joined consisted only of Chief Rankin, Sergeant Brown, and two constables, Cummins and Hayden. When Constable Hayden left, the force was once again brought up to five by Eric Elwell. Chief Rankin was the only one with a car. Sergeant Brown had a push bike, and the constables, including Joe Bull, used motorcycles.

Each man was allotted only one day and one night off a week, and there was always the chance that this time off might be cancelled if a special event demanded that everyone be on duty. Even when off duty, Joe had to be within answering distance of a telephone at all times, and holidays were non-existent. Winter was especially unpleasant, driving miles on his motorcycle in miserable conditions.

By 1938, Joe Bull was made police chief and the force had become somewhat more modernized with a second car added for the sergeant. Two more cars in each of the years 1940 and 1941 increased the numbers, and a two-way radio was also installed in 1941, making the policeman's lot a far happier one. The Saanich police force was greatly enlarged by the end of the Second World War, and in 1950 the three-shift system came into effect, so that each man had an equal amount of duty and time off.

Chief Joe Bull was said to have been one of the kindest men imaginable by all who knew him. Both rich and poor were numbered among his friends and, in his office at the police station, it was said that one could just as easily find a pedlar as the lieutenant-governor himself. He treated everyone equally and, in his opinion, there was no such thing as a bad person.

Joe retired in 1957 to the original five acres of the old Bull farm which he and his wife had retained. One of their four children, daughter Joyce, worked in the premier's office.

People long remembered Joe as one of the best men the police force ever had. He had an inborn gift for public relations, enabling him to easily converse with people from all stations in life. Following his death in 1965 at the age of sixty-nine, his widow Gladys lived on in the old manor house on Quadra until her own death at the age of eighty-five in 1985.

4201 Quadra Street

762 RALPH STREET

THE HOUSE THAT FINALLY MOVED

Through the years many people wondered why the big, yellow house in the oasis of green on Saanich Road near the Town & Country Shopping Centre remained on its site despite all the changes going on around it. Other houses in the neighbourhood were being demolished or moved to make room for commercial development, but this particular house stayed.

The owner of the house at the time was Louis Pedneault, a man of conviction and strong principles. He was proud of his two-storey, 3,200-square-foot landmark home, and felt his decision to hold on to it was nobody's business but his own so, despite extensive real estate pressure, he refused to sell. For sixty-one years the Pedneault house remained precisely where Lou Pedneault had built it in 1938, and looked much the same as it always had. New development and noisy traffic began to encroach on his property but he remained firm in his conviction. The house was not for sale.

He perhaps remembered a time when his land was covered with many oak trees, and pheasant had roamed the area. In the beginning there was only one other house opposite his property and the old train tracks ran up Short Street to the rear. It was pleasant countryside.

Joseph Louis Pedneault was born in La Broquerie, Manitoba, in 1902, to Alfred and Emma (Dubreuil) Pedneault. There were eventually six sons and three daughters in the family and in 1906 they decided to move west and settle in Victoria where the nine children grew up. Lou later met Kathleen Lillian Painter and the two were married in 1926 when he was twenty-four and she just seventeen.

The young couple moved first to Los Angeles where Lou learned the trade of plastering, but when they returned to Victoria to attend brother Joe Pedneault's wedding, they decided to stay on Vancouver Island and settle in Sooke. Lou and Joe formed a partnership in the logging business, logging various areas in Sooke and Mill Bay and supplying MacMillan's seven small mills. They made approximately $6 per thousand board feet, floating the logs downriver to the mills, and as they could not afford to hire labour in the beginning, their wives worked for them.

An injury to his hand meant Lou eventually had to sell his logging business and he then headed north up the island in the mid-1930s. Again in business with his brothers, Lou chose the isolation of Zeballos on the west coast, and it was there that the Pedneaults made the wisest investment of their lives. They agreed to furnish trucks and road-building equipment to a newly established mining camp, and in exchange for rental fees and wages, they accepted shares in the soon-to-be famous Privateer Mine.

Once the Pedneault brothers had established a road to the mine and a cook was hired for the new camp, the number one vein began producing rich, high-grade ore. Things continued to go well which encouraged the men to purchase more steel and powder and, although there was still insufficient money

762 Ralph Street

to pay wages, everyone continued to draw shares in the mine. A Toronto company became interested in the property and the shares skyrocketed overnight. Within a few months, shares in the original syndicate, which had once been worthless, were now $5 each.

It was indeed a profitable time for Lou Pedneault and his family, but it was also a hard, pioneering life in those days. Living conditions for women and children in such a remote area were difficult.

Between 1936 and 1938, over 9,000 tons of crude ore were shipped from Zeballos to a Tacoma smelter, and over the coming years the ore returned 168,318 ounces of gold and 68,589 ounces of silver, worth well over $6,000,000.

Lou Pedneault had been lucky and perhaps this was the reason for his later stubbornness about selling the house in Victoria which had been built from his gains. He had paid his dues and earned his money with blood, sweat, tears and a touch of luck.

He returned to Victoria in 1937, purchased acreage from the Tolmie family in Saanich and then set about building his dream house, most of which he did himself. Horses and a plough were used to dig out the driveway ready for the cement to be poured. A family member, Jules Demurs, and some day labour assisted with the work. The house was originally stuccoed in grey but was later changed to a yellowish-beige.

It was a sturdily built house and very well insulated. Oak floors were laid throughout with sturdy, multi-coloured linoleum gracing the kitchen and bathroom floors. Blackboards were installed on the walls of the basement playroom for Lou's four daughters, Louise, Dorothy, Jeanette and Antoinette. Interior furnishings came from Mac & Mac's furniture store on Government Street in Victoria. Very few changes were made to the house through the years. Even the 1938 paint was original.

Lou didn't change either. He was still the same down-to-earth, somewhat gruff man, who liked to tease his daughters. He enjoyed working in the basement on his many projects and even on Christmas Day was reluctant to wash and get dressed up, preferring his old greasy work clothes. He also built other houses in the Victoria area, carrying his tools around in his old Packard with the back seat removed.

The Pedneault house was always full of people. During the Second World War when Lou served as a warden, he often brought home servicemen from Naden to stay with the family. All were treated to his wife's hospitality and good cooking. Mrs. Pedneault's breakfasts were legendary. She frequently served up to twenty people at the large dining table. With four daughters, and eventually fourteen grandchildren and thirteen great-grandchildren, plus their many friends, it was hardly surprising that the house was rarely quiet.

In January of 1997, Lou Pedneault passed away, and two years later the property was finally sold, but the house itself was saved from demolition. Instead, it was moved to a new site on Ralph Street overlooking the Swan Lake nature sanctuary by the current owners, Brad and Tracy Shuya, who are today equally dedicated to preserving its heritage.

3808 HERITAGE LANE

THE CAPTAIN ROBERT WALKER HOUSE

Tucked away up Heritage Lane, an offshoot of Burnside Road West, sits the residence, and part-time bed-and-breakfast, of Sandra and Larry Gray.

Over the past decade, this charming home, known initially as the "Captain Walker house," has been thoroughly transformed by the Grays. With an enormous amount of "blood, sweat and tears," they have successfully managed to preserve its beauty and elegance. Their extensive work since 1990 has included gutting rooms, knocking out walls, stripping floors, painting, stained-glass window work, and other incidentals, all of which earned them a Heritage Award of Merit from the Hallmark Society in 1999.

The Grays, who previously lived in Los Angeles, have had a long-time love affair with heritage homes and strongly believe in the importance of preservation. The Captain Walker house was an enormous challenge for them, but one they enjoyed immensely.

"It is strange but there were so many connections to our own life in the Walker house," Sandra Gray said, "so obviously our buying it and getting involved in its restoration was meant to be!" She was referring specifically to her interest in arts-and-crafts and all Japanese-influenced decor, so when she later learned the history of the house and that Captain Walker himself also had many connections with Japan which he had incorporated into his home, she was amazed.

The adventurous Captain Robert Walker, who built the house around 1915, was born into a seafaring family in Maryport, Cumberland, England, in 1851. Both Robert and his older brother, Wilson, were influenced by their marine family ancestry and went to sea at a young age.

By 1874, Robert was chief officer on the *Horai-Maru,* a Mitsubishi Steamship Company vessel, under the command of brother Wilson. Two years later he received his own commander's licence from the Japanese government and took over the *Heian-Maru.* In 1877 he was decorated by the Japanese government for helping to quash the Satsuma Rebellion.

By this time he had fallen in love with the beautiful Sato Fukuda. Although he did not officially marry her until 1886, they had lived together since the 1870s, and had moved to a western-style home overlooking Nagasaki harbour. Walker took over control of the *Takachiho-Maru* following the formation of Nippon Yusen Kaisha (NYK). Through the coming years, he and Sato had nine children.

In 1891, Walker quit NYK and took his family back to England where tragically, in 1894, Sato died of heart disease at the young age of thirty-six. She lies buried in Cumberland. A broken-hearted Walker decided to return to Japan the following year with his children, and then established R.N. Walker & Co. (stevedores and ship chandlers) in Nagasaki, a place which reminded him of his wife.

In 1908, however, he was once again on the move, this time to Canada, leaving his son, Robert junior, to run the company in Japan. Upon arrival on

Vancouver Island, he acquired land on Burnside Road West, first building the house at number 1245. The Canadian Northern Pacific Railway purchased the house from him in 1915, and he moved to his ten-acre property to the north where he built the house that now stands on Heritage Lane.

Walker designed the floor plans himself, but the exterior elevations were designed by architect Elmer E. Green, and the house was built by a Mr. Gerard. In 1928, Walker sold the house to Helena Von Holstein-Rathlou, the wife of a Danish count, and moved to Hollywood Crescent. He died shortly before his ninetieth birthday in 1941, and is buried in Royal Oak Cemetery.

Owners of the house after the count's wife sold it in 1942 include the Piddingtons, the Mortels, the Stangs, and the Gilberts. The Mortels divided up the original ten acres, and further subdividing in the 1980s reduced the property to a little over an acre. Today "Heritage House," with its attractive California bungalow-style decor and large veranda and balustrade columns in front, still stands proud, despite the invasion of newer homes surrounding it.

One of Robert and Sato's daughters, Kate, married Hubert Cumberbirch, one-time teacher at Victoria High School. Violet, another daughter, had a career in Hollywood before settling in Penticton. Of the other daughters, Maud was a nurse during the First World War, and Annie married a U.S. trade commissioner. The Walker family history and their connection to Nagasaki has been compiled in a book by a Canadian writer, Brian Burke-Gaffney.

No heritage house seems complete without a ghost story. Sandra Gray, a level-headed lady, reluctantly admits that her house is no exception. She has often experienced a presence in the house, and once awoke to see the image of someone smoking a pipe beside her bed – Captain Walker? Another apparition was of a small woman in white with arms outstretched. Could this be Sato Walker? Other guests at her home have had similar experiences. Sandra has a theory that the late Mrs. Walker might not be happy that she is buried in England far away from her husband in Canada and "visits" the house occasionally to express her displeasure.

Nonetheless, bed-and-breakfast guests through the years, who include a senator from Delaware, a travel writer, an undercover narcotics agent, a priest and a fire chief from Austin, Texas, all agree with the Grays that the so-called "ghostly presence" is friendly and seems delighted that so much love and care have been put back into Captain Robert Walker's home on Heritage Lane.

3808 Heritage Lane

588 RIDGEGROVE AVENUE

THE PIONEERING FAGERBERGS

The recent deaths of sisters Clara and Elsa Fagerberg, last remaining members of the Fagerberg family of the Wilkinson Road area, emphasize the significant role pioneers played in the early development of Greater Victoria, and how important it is to document their histories.

Clara Fagerberg was born in Winnipeg, Manitoba, in October of 1907, and came to Victoria with her parents, Bertha and Oscar Fagerberg, in 1913. The Fagerberg roots were in Sweden but Bertha's father, Theodore Nelson, already owned property along Wilkinson Road and it was there that his daughter and son-in-law, Oscar, began to build their one-and- a-half-storey, gabled house, which was to become the family home for over seven decades.

By 1921 the house was finally completed with porches, a dormer, and multi-paned casement windows. That same year, tragedy struck the family when Oscar, working in the garden, was bitten by a spider, had an allergic reaction, and died. By the time of his death, two other children had joined the Fagerberg family, another daughter, Elsa, and a son, George.

George Fagerberg was later well known in the area as the long-time manager of Layritz Nurseries. His two sisters, Clara and Elsa, were very well loved in the community for their church work at Grace Lutheran Church, at one time situated at Queens and Blanshard. Both sisters sang in the choir there and every week took flowers from the garden of their Ridgegrove home to decorate the church. On the occasion of Saanich municipality's seventy-fifth anniversary in 1981, both sisters were presented with badges for having, at that time, been residents of Saanich for over fifty years.

During their lifetimes, the two Fagerberg ladies took frequent trips which they called their "holiday adventures." Some of the trips led them back to their roots in Sweden, but most were automobile trips across North America with Clara driving and Elsa acting as navigator.

Although neither woman ever married, they both had a great love for children and enjoyed baking cookies for all the neighbourhood youngsters as well as their friends. Clara attended Victoria High School, followed by time at Sprott Shaw College, where she learned office and secretarial skills. She then worked for many years at Smith, Davidson & Leckey, a wholesale paper company. She was also a talented potter, a needlepoint specialist, and a professional seamstress.

At the time of Clara's death, she had lived eighty-five of her ninety years in the house her father had built. She had just celebrated her ninetieth birthday in the Gorge Road Hospital surrounded by all those who loved her. The nurses had dressed her in her Sunday best for the occasion, and balloons and cake were the order of the day. Sister Elsa resided for a short while in another seniors' residence in Saanich until her death shortly thereafter.

Some years earlier, while the sisters were still living in the family home, the original acreage was subdivided and other homes built nearby. Today, the

588 Ridgegrove Avenue

Fagerberg house is no longer family owned and is currently rented. When a family friend helped clean the house and pack up belongings following the deaths of the two sisters, numerous Swedish newspapers were found packed away in the basement, as well as a great deal of other memorabilia from a different culture and time.

931 WOODHALL DRIVE

THE ROGERS FARMING TRADITION LIVES ON

The house which today stands at 931 Woodhall Drive off Quadra Street was built by pioneer farmer George Rogers in 1925.

Rogers was an adventurous man who had emigrated to Canada from Cheshire, England, in 1885, and was determined to make his mark in the New World. A brief stop in Toronto where he worked for a while in a hat factory convinced him he should continue to head west. His journey to Vancouver was made on one of the first trains to travel across the continent from sea to sea.

He arrived in Victoria with a background in farming and milling and worked for the first year on Medina Farm in James Bay. He then became a tenant farmer for Stuart Yates at Craigie Lea Farm at the corner of Tillicum and Gorge. There he turned his talents to dairy farming.

By 1898, George and his new wife, Lillie Stevens, had saved enough money to purchase Alderley Farm on Agnes Street which occupied land east of Glanford Avenue and west of Quadra Street. This land had previously been farmed by the Vanalman family. George later changed the name of the farm to "Chester Lea" and eventually his property extended to over 250 acres. The original Rogers farmhouse was still in existence until the 1970s when it was finally demolished.

Much of the Rogers acreage was uncleared bush land that Rogers paid Chinese labour to cut and clear. Some of these men had previously worked on the construction of the Canadian Pacific Railway across the Rockies.

The old Victoria and Sidney Railway ran through the Rogers land, quite near the original farmhouse. The engine frequently belched out smoke and red-hot cinders as it passed by and this became quite a problem during the hot, dry summer months when bush fires were a common occurrence.

The Rogers family continued to be successful cattle farmers for many years and numerous deals were cut at the farm or on Saturday mornings at the cattle auction in the market yard between Cormorant and Fisgard streets.

Soon after Lillie Rogers' death in 1925, a second farmhouse was built for George senior and his two daughters, Rosa Ethel and Beatrice, and this is the house that stands on Woodhall Drive today. George's brother, Joseph, did the decorative carving to be found on the living-room fireplace. The handrail to the basement is made of redwood.

In those days, there was no Woodhall Drive and the land surrounding the house down towards Quadra Street was covered in wildflowers. To the rear of the house, which was then the front, cows grazed in fields as far as the eye could see. A story passed down through the Rogers family states that on one occasion one of the many pheasants roaming the neighbourhood inadvertently flew into the dining-room window, killing itself in the process. The window had to be replaced but a pheasant dinner was enjoyed by the family that night.

George senior passed away in 1943 and son George and his wife, Genevieve, moved into the house and carried on the family dairy business until it finally closed down in 1958. George junior was on the milk round every day from 1920 until 1958. One of George junior's daughters, Phyllis, married Richard Fatt. The Fatts were well-known chicken farmers.

George senior's daughter, Rosa Ethel, who never married, was a victim of polio. She lived on at the Woodhall Drive house until her own death in 1967. To supplement her income during those years, she used her talents as an artist to paint wildflowers on greeting cards and calendars. In addition, she did all the bookkeeping for the family dairy business.

Between 1967 and 1978, the house was rented but then, with the development of much of the Rogers' acreage well under way, Steve and Marilyn Norman purchased the old house which had been scheduled for demolition. At that time it was still approached from Rogers Avenue, as the subdivision off Quadra Street had not yet been put through and there was no proper road leading up to the house. The move was horrendous for the Normans because their two daughters had chicken pox at the time. All their furniture had to be brought in by truck across the field behind the house. On the day of the move, the house was being insulated through holes which had not been covered over inside, and consequently insulation was spread everywhere throughout the house. Marilyn Norman, who had always had a passion for heritage houses, wondered just what they had let themselves in for, and began to understand why the house had been considered for demolition once the new subdivision went through.

Slowly, however, under the Normans' care, the house began to take shape with various alterations and renovations, turning the old Rogers' farmhouse back into a delightfully warm, family home. More recently, some tasteful heritage cosmetic painting has added to the house's charm.

The Rogers family and their farming traditions are still remembered in the area by roads which are named for family members such as Lily Avenue (spelled differently from George senior's wife, Lillie) and Genevieve Road. Chesterlea Road is named for the original Rogers farm, and Rogers Avenue commemorates the whole family.

931 Woodhall Drive

1248 BURNSIDE ROAD WEST

A SIMPLE COTTAGE OR A GRAND LODGE?

In May 1992, a small cottage, affectionately known as "Hall Cottage" in memory of its original owners, and its surrounding garden on Burnside Road West, was designated as a heritage site.

The following spring, however, the cottage, with some of its windows boarded up, was awaiting its fate and the word "demolition" was being bandied about in order to make way for a parking lot adjacent to Knockan Hill Park. A great deal of volunteer work by a very dedicated group of people known as the Friends of Knockan Hill (created in December 1990) managed to save the cottage from this fate and allowed it to continue to survive in its charming woodland setting.

More recently, the cottage has reverted to its original, grander name, "Stranton Lodge," and the Saanich Heritage Foundation has taken over its management with the creation of the Stranton Lodge Management Committee composed of volunteer representatives from the Friends of Knockan Hill, the Strawberry Vale Ratepayers Association and the Strawberry Vale Community Affairs Association. Together with the Saanich Heritage Foundation, these volunteers were successful in obtaining funds so that work on the cottage could be carried out to once again make it habitable and secure from further deterioration. A second plan went into operation in 1995 to restore the unique gardens surrounding Stranton Lodge to their former glory.

The cottage was built in 1930 for Thomas and Maude Hall who were both born in Hartlepool, County Durham, England, in 1882. They arrived in Canada in 1911 and 1912 respectively, met and married in Vancouver, and eventually settled in Saanich on Loenholm Road in 1913.

Thomas Hall was a teacher and later principal of George Jay School, and then became the inspector of schools. By the 1930s, the Halls had asked their friend, Hubert Savage, to design a house for them on Burnside Road, and Hall Cottage, built by Donald Lindsay, was the result. In a charming English arts and crafts style, the cottage was situated in a woodland setting with a fieldstone foundation, stuccoed walls and rustic weatherboards in the gables. The windows were diamond-paned leaded lights.

The Halls were exceptional gardeners and their garden soon became a showplace in Saanich. It was sculpted out of the rocks with a series of cascading pools and springs, and steps descending the steep slope. Flower beds were planted with special regard to a natural woodland setting.

Thomas Hall retired in 1954 and died in 1962, but his wife lived on in the cottage until 1973 at which time she sold her three hectares of woodland, including her house and garden, to the people of Saanich. She then moved into a nursing home where she died in 1985 at age 103. On May 10, 1984, one year before she died, Mrs. Hall wrote a letter to the mayor and council of Saanich stating:

1248 Burnside Road West

> Now my house and land belong to Saanich and I hope that many people will enjoy the lower park and care for it lovingly.

The history of Stranton Lodge dates back to the 1930s, but the use of its surrounding parkland goes back many centuries to a time when the Songhees harvested camas below the Garry oaks and firs on Knockan Hill. In the 1850s, Scottish settlers at Craigflower Farm first brought the Scots Gaelic word *gnocan* meaning "knoll" or "hill" to Victoria, and in 1858 an official map showed George McKenzie as purchaser of some sixty acres north of Portage Inlet on the east slope of Knockan Hill.

Knockan Hill was mentioned again in 1885 on the J.D. Pemberton map of southeast Vancouver Island, and in 1906 four hectares of the hilltop at Knockan Hill became public land in the newly incorporated municipality of Saanich. In 1989 Knockan Hill Park was officially preserved by a by-law and, with a further one acre added in 1993, is now a community park.

Today, Stranton Lodge is rented and, as such, is private property, but the gardens and the surrounding park are open for the public to enjoy. The goals of the Friends of Knockan Hill Park Society today are simply to protect and preserve the park's wilderness character and to generate public respect for the flora and fauna therein. In essence, the society is carrying out the wishes of the Halls who wanted their house and land to be enjoyed and cared for in perpetuity.

THE DORIS PAGE HOUSE

A COTTAGE IN THE WOODS AND A LEGENDARY LADY

The intriguing 1920s cottage that once stood at the corner of Haliburton Road and Lochside Drive was occupied for almost half a century by a delightful lady called Doris Page, a horticultural genius and a fascinating character. The small Cordova Bay park opposite her property was named for this woman in 1989 as a result of her diligence in trying to keep the area in a natural, park-like state for the benefit and enjoyment of the people of Cordova Bay.

The Doris Page Winter Garden at the Horticultural Centre of the Pacific is also named in her honour. She had an unassuming manner and modest demeanour and was, therefore, somewhat surprised by these tributes. She imagined one had to die before one had things named after oneself. Nonetheless, her contributions to the world of horticulture in Greater Victoria had rightfully earned her these accolades.

Doris Page was born in England and trained in horticulture in Warwickshire. When she arrived in Canada in 1948 she could not understand why her gardening talents were such a novelty – after all, she had come from a country of gardeners. Miss Page soon found a job working for Ed Lohbrunner at his Lakeview Gardens nursery on Blenkinsop Road, and was initially paid the princely sum of 50 cents an hour. She stayed with Lohbrunner's nursery for the next thirty-two years (with suitable pay increases), and during that time also had her own gardening show on CHEK TV called "Island Country Garden," which she enjoyed for over eighteen years.

Doris Page moved into her woodland cottage in 1949 soon after her arrival in Victoria. The craftsman-style cottage had been built in the 1920s for George and Ernest Hick and was a former summer cottage only, with several additions through the years. A full-length veranda on the east side of the building was later enclosed with glass.

The first time Miss Page visited the cottage, she and her faithful spaniel had just come from a swim in the bay. They climbed up the slope to the cottage nestled serenely in the woods, and she was enchanted by its magical appearance.

Even by the 1990s nothing much had changed. A visit to the cottage was like stepping back in time. The steep, winding driveway led up to the cottage which suddenly and unexpectedly appeared through the trees beyond the rose trellis and small patio. Wildflowers bordered the path and birds sang from their perches in overhanging trees.

It was rather like venturing into a fairy tale. Knocking on the front door one half-expected it to be opened by a manifestation of the Fairy Godmother or even perhaps the Wicked Witch.

Doris Page died on January 29, 1999, and in the fall of 2000 her cottage in the woods was demolished for reasons of deterioration. Sadly, it was not considered worthy of saving as a heritage piece.

But Doris Page and her small woodland home will not soon be forgotten. The Saanich Parks Department plans on turning her garden into a picnic area as part of the Doris Page Park together with an interpretive centre on the site of her house, acknowledging this lady's many important horticultural works in the municipality.

(We decided to include the Doris Page cottage in this collection before it was demolished. Although it disappeared during the production of this book, the cottage was left in for sentimental reasons.)

975 Haliburton Road

600 SEACLIFFE ROAD

A MANOR HOUSE

When Clare and Dennis Atkinson became the owners of a turn-of-the-century house on the Saanich Peninsula in 1999, they embarked on an adventure of discovery. Unravelling the history of their home is ongoing, and fascinating new discoveries continue to come to light.

The story of "Arncliffe Manor," as it was once known, and its surrounding acreage, dates back to August of 1883. Businessman Jacob Hunter Todd purchased 132 acres of virgin land on the peninsula that year, near where the house now stands. Todd logged his acreage, made some money, and then sold most of his land a few months later. He did, however, donate some of it, as did subsequent owners, for park area, and today a section of his original acreage forms part of John Dean Park.

Over the years, the acreage continued to shrink in size, and today the Atkinsons' house stands on approximately one acre of the original land. The house is believed to have been built there some time between 1907 and 1911. Although its style is most definitely like that of Samuel Maclure, the owners have as yet been unable to confirm who designed and built the house. Even information on its name, Arncliffe Manor, is somewhat sketchy, and when they first moved in, the Atkinsons thought of coming up with another name for their home. They did, however, recently discover that some neighbourhood children had unearthed an old steel sign nearby with the name Arncliffe Manor inscribed on it. When the children built a tree house on their own property, they placed the elegant sign at its entrance, giving it a rather grand moniker. The Atkinsons are hoping one day to return the sign to where it rightfully belongs.

Todd sold his land in April of 1884 to Robert Garnett Tatlow who, in turn, sold to Charles Jones. On July 21, 1898, Harrison Garside was listed as property owner, but by May 1 of 1907, ownership was in the name of Caroline Elizabeth White Birch and at some point while the land was in her possession, the house was built.

By 1911, the house had a new owner, Robert Dunsmuir Bryden, a grandson of Robert Dunsmuir. Bryden's mother was Elizabeth Dunsmuir who had married John Bryden in 1867. Following an article written about the house in 1999, a nephew of Robert Bryden came by to visit the Atkinsons and added to the memories: during his uncle's ownership a Chinese cook resided there; another of Bryden's nephews occasionally acted as Bryden's chauffeur. Mr. Bryden owned a Packard and he or his nephew could often be seen driving it around the neighbourhood.

Cora McMicken and Elizabeth Emily McFeeley purchased the house next from the Bryden estate, and Harold Cross was yet another owner. The Atkinsons acquired the house in 1999 through a court-ordered sale and it was vacant when they took occupancy. By then the house and grounds had sadly deteriorated and everything needed a great deal of work. One of the broken windows had enabled a family of bats to take up residence inside.

600 Seacliffe Road

While Clare continued to delve into the house's history, Dennis was busy on the grounds clearing away trees and undergrowth. He re-roofed the house, and a cottage and stables also on the property. Four layers of roofing material had to be removed, an amount weighing in at twenty-five tons. A battle then ensued with a barrage of carpenter ants which had invaded many areas of these structures.

Slowly, however, things began to take shape and the beauty and former glory of this elegant manor house came alive. The interior has now had some cosmetic touches, as wallpaper has been removed and, with the assistance of a colour consultant, walls have been painted in soft green with white trim, giving a definite heritage ambience. The carpets have been lifted in the large living room – facetiously nicknamed "the ballroom" because of its enormous size – and an exciting discovery was made. The centre of the hardwood floor appeared to be lighter in shade, giving rise to the theory that it was indeed once specifically used for dancing with the carpet just covering the perimeter of the floor. More information pieced together from past owners and long-ago visitors to the house has enabled the Atkinsons to identify other alterations to the house.

Dennis Atkinson has continued to clear trees on his property and has now completed renovations to the pool area. While digging in the grounds, he found numerous old bottles, mostly English port, as well as pieces of china. Underneath the garage, which once housed the Bryden Packard, 1930s antifreeze cans have been located.

The original entrance to the manor house was from the 8500 block of West Saanich Road and there the old stone entrance pillars can still be seen at the top of the long circular driveway which once led to the property. Today, the elegant manor house is reached from Seacliffe Road.

BABBACOMBE FARM

HARRODS AND HOLSTEINS

Who would suspect a connection between the esteemed institution known as Harrods in London, and a Saanich farmhouse on Hunt Road at the intersection with Dooley?

The farmhouse in question is an elegant Tudor-revival building built between 1912 and 1916 for an Englishman named Herbert Burbidge. Burbidge once worked for the London department store and his father, Sir Richard Burbidge, was managing director of Harrods from 1891 until 1916, transforming the business during those years by adding more departments and, by 1902, increasing the staff to approximately 2,000.

Son Herbert Burbidge, however, left the business and came to Canada in 1910 to become the store commissioner for the Hudson's Bay Company in Victoria. He was the man largely responsible for "The Bay" as it is known today on Douglas Street.

In 1921 Herbert retired to his Hunt Road property which he called "Babbacombe Farm" in memory of his English roots, delighting in its typically English farmhouse appearance. The one-storey section of the house on the east side is thought to have been built originally as a summer cottage in 1912, with the remainder, designed by Henry Gillingham, added in 1916.

Between 1945 and 1956, the property was owned by Harold Brooks, who bred Jersey cattle on the farm. Following Brooks, the 120-acre farm was owned and run by the Youell family. The Youells began breeding their first Holstein cattle on the acreage in 1961. These black-and-white cattle, originating in the Netherlands and dating back some 2,000 years in that region to the time of Julius Caesar, are certainly one of the oldest known type of dairy cattle. The Youells were the first to foster the development of Holsteins on Vancouver Island and proudly earned the Master Breeder Shield for their efforts.

In the year 2000, the property was acquired by the Fatt family who, since moving in, have upgraded the plumbing and electrical work and also raised the house to make a full basement beneath. They still retain twenty-five acres where today they breed beef cattle, and the Fatts' son, Wayne, who has built a house on the property, farms a further twenty-eight acres of land. With the recent sale of another chunk of original Youell land, the entire farm is now under new ownership.

Charles Henry Harrod, the founder of the Harrods store in London, and a miller by trade, would no doubt have been suitably impressed by his employees' Canadian connections. He founded the store in 1849 initially as a simple grocery which specialized in the import and sale of tea. In 1861, Harrod's son, Charles Digby Harrod, expanded Harrods with a wide range of goods including furniture, perfume, china and glass. When Charles retired in 1889, the business was floated as a limited company, but retained the prestigious family name: Harrods Stores Limited.

Two years later, the new managing director, Richard Burbidge, acquired much of the land surrounding the store and was able to carry out an expansion plan. By 1911, Harrods was firmly established as the world's most famous department store with its gourmet food items and high fashion, and was boasting the best circulating library in London at the time.

The store also claimed that customers could use their services not only for purchasing the most unusual of merchandise, but also for buying theatre tickets, making travel reservations and arranging funerals.

Newspaper headlines over the years have told the story of Harrods with items entitled "Harrods Wooing Shoppers with its New Moving Staircase" in 1898, and "Harrods Reaching 10 Million People with Wireless Broadcasts" in 1925. Then, in 1959, Harrods was the subject of a takeover bid launched by the Scottish company, the House of Fraser. In 1985, the Al Fayed Investment and Trust (UK) Limited acquired the House of Fraser for $615 million. Today, Harrods chairman, Mohamed Al Fayed, father of Dodi Fayed, Princess Diana's companion who died alongside her in the tragic Paris car crash in 1997, describes his store simply as "my palace in Knightsbridge."

However, the son of one of the early men responsible for making Harrods what it is today, could quite easily have also described his farming business on Vancouver Island, Babbacombe Farm, as his own particular palace on the Saanich Peninsula.

6187 Hunt Road

NORFOLK LODGE

THE OLDFIELD STORY

One of Samuel Maclure's most impressive houses is situated in rural Saanich on Brookhill Road. Known as "Norfolk Lodge," it was built by the Oldfield family in 1908, two years after purchasing approximately 300 acres in the Elk Lake district.

John Henry Oldfield, son of a wealthy Englishman, hailed from Norfolk, England, hence the name he later chose for his home. At the age of twenty-two he was sent by his father to oversee the family's sugar plantations in Jamaica but sickness brought on by the intense heat eventually forced him to leave and head for Canada in 1879. He settled in Winnipeg where he prospered in real estate before heading west to Vancouver Island.

The Oldfields were not the first owners of the land they purchased. Randle Caesar from California had been an earlier owner, as had James Holroyd who acquired the property in 1893. When the Oldfields bought the land around 1906, there were still the remains of kilns on the acreage that had once been used for making charcoal. Because of the many trees, John's son, Clarence Oldfield, with a Chinese friend named Quinn, spent the next two years clearing the land in order to build their mansion.

When both the senior Oldfields died in the 1920s, son Clarence and his wife Doris moved into Norfolk Lodge and hired Maclure to redesign the house. Bay windows, a wide veranda and an upstairs gallery were then added, as well as rough-cut ashlar masonry, an observation tower and some interior panelling. For the next twenty years, Clarence and Doris shared the home with Clarence's sister, Kathleen, and the land was run as a hobby farm until 1948, when the property was sold. The Oldfields then became residents of the Oak Bay Beach Hotel. Doris Oldfield died in 1953 and Clarence moved to the home of his widowed daughter-in-law in Royal Oak. He died at the age of seventy-six in 1966, leaving four children.

But Clarence Oldfield's influence on the Saanich community had been notable. Very active in local affairs, he was one of the founders of the Saanich Fruit Growers' Association and was its president for a number of years. He also helped start the Growers Wine Company as well as being active in civic affairs as both a councillor (1924 to 1930) and reeve of Saanich.

In addition, he was the prime instigator encouraging members of the community to invest in the land which later became the Royal Oak Burial Park. A man of vision, he could see the need for such a cemetery because of the growing population and he felt that churchyards would soon become obsolete as burial sites. Clarence's oldest son, Herbert, later joined the church as a minister, first in Manitoba and then in England, moving back to Vancouver Island in 1979.

In December of 1929, a decaying fir tree north of Norfolk Lodge and west of the intersection of Brookleigh and Oldfield was felled by hand by three men. This 229-foot-tall tree was well over 300 years old and the trunk, measuring

5789 Brookhill Road

over thirty-five feet in circumference, yielded thirty-four cords of wood. This was enough to heat Norfolk Lodge for a year. A section of this massive tree was sent to the old Saanich Municipal Hall at Royal Oak and remained there for thirty years until 1960. Then, for some years, it stood on the porch of the old Pioneer Museum in Saanichton until finally it was brought to the new Saanich Municipal Hall on Vernon Avenue.

Another branch of the Oldfield family through John Henry's cousin, Horace, also made their mark on Vancouver Island. Horace arrived in 1895 at the age of eighteen. Within a year of his arrival, he had also acquired land in the Prospect Lake area. There he kept poultry and planted a large orchard. In 1935, his two sons, Basil and Brian, built the garage at 5295 West Saanich Road.

Basil Oldfield (known as Barney) was the inventor in this branch of the family. He designed and built the unique, twelve-sided house at 5321 Old West Saanich Road. Constructed on a motorized shaft, the house is able to turn a full 360 degrees. When Barney died in 1978, the cupola was still incomplete. His many other inventions and designs included a specialized logging truck, bulldozer blades, and a custom-built car called the "Spirit of Tomorrow."

Through two different branches of the same family, the Oldfields certainly left their stamp in the Saanich area. Norfolk Lodge, their most visible memorial, has had many different owners through the years since the Oldfields, and has benefitted from a considerable amount of renovation work to preserve its heritage.

THE CURRIE MISSION HOUSE

SCHOONERS, MISSIONS AND A BARBER SHOP

The present structure at 4794 West Saanich Road is the third building to stand on that site, and is totally different in design from its two predecessors.

Standing two and half storeys high, the wing that faces the West Saanich Road even housed a barber's shop for many years. The house's most important claim to heritage fame, however, is that for approximately three years, from 1912 to 1915, it was inhabited by a retired missionary, the Reverend Walter T. Currie and his wife, Amy, who renamed the house "Chissamba" in memory of the village in Africa where he had worked for twenty-five years.

Today, a stone marker and plaque stands in front of the house on the West Saanich Road near the intersection of Beaver Lake Road. The marker was unveiled on Sunday, 23 May, 1937, in memory of this very special Saanich resident and his missionary work which was compared at the ceremony to that of David Livingstone. The unveiling was attended by such notables as Saanich reeve, William Crouch, Dr. J. S. Plaskett of the Dominion Astrophysical Observatory and Dr. Willard Brewing, president of the United Church Conference, as well as a crowd of almost 400.

Although Currie's missionary work seemed to have been forgotten after his death on April 7, 1915, a major effort was made by the United Church twenty-two years later to immortalize this man and his important work in the field. The church obtained a small piece of land from the owners of the West Saanich Road house and then bore the expense for the memorial plaque. Since then, the house has always been known as the "Currie Mission House."

The history of that section of land, however, dates back to the 1850s when John Stevens, a young man from Kent in England who had apprenticed as a seaman and then inherited a trading schooner from his uncle, settled down on Vancouver Island. Prior to 1859, he had plied the west coast of North America from San Francisco to Vancouver Island but in 1850, having married Georgina Holmes, a widow with a young son, he thought it was time to put down some roots.

He acquired section 106 on the West Saanich Road and by 1861 had built the first of his three hotels which he called the "Half-Way House," probably because it stood exactly half way between Victoria and Tod Inlet. In 1890, this hotel burned to the ground.

The second hotel was simply called the "Stevens Hotel" and was similar in shape and style to the original. The third hotel, which is the building standing there today, was built in 1898. This hotel was apparently a popular destination for honeymoon couples.

John Stevens had by then retired and moved to a house on Goward Road because his wife had decided that living above a saloon was not a good environment for raising her children. Her eldest son, David, took over the running of the Stevens Hotel but, by the turn of the twentieth century, there were other, more popular, hotels in the area such as the Royal Oak Inn and the Swan

Lake Hotel, so Stevens decided to turn his hotel into a farm and renamed the house "Westwood." He specialized in fruit growing and was quite successful for a while. In 1907, however, he sold the land and moved to James Bay. His father, John Stevens, had earlier donated some of their land for St. Michael and All Angels' Church nearby.

And then, for three short years, the house was home to the Reverend Currie, perhaps its most important occupant. In addition to the marker and plaque which commemorates his work, further posthumous honours were bestowed upon Currie in December 1950 when Frederico Mussili, the first graduate of the Currie Institute in Angola, laid a wreath on the marker in memory of this great man.

The Currie Mission House is designated as heritage in the Saanich inventory of homes and, as such, has successfully managed to avoid demolition on numerous occasions. The current owners are presently restoring the house to its former glory.

4794 West Saanich Road

Oak Bay

Oak Bay councillor and reeve Francis Mawson Rattenbury, who was also one of Victoria's most famous architects, once said of Oak Bay that it "is one of the most lovely residential areas I have ever seen, and it is my desire to retain this beauty as far as possible."

Ninety-five years after incorporation as a municipality, Oak Bay has indeed managed to retain that appeal and has become one of the most interesting areas in Greater Victoria. Perhaps the secret formula behind the success of the proverbial "Tweed Curtain" is that Oak Bay has become a municipality of note while still retaining a relatively small population (around 18,000).

In addition, a combination of age groups (seniors as well as young families) living in the municipality has allowed Oak Bay to preserve a mix of housing styles, so that today the grandest of mansions owned by the wealthy and more modest accommodations can all be found within the borders of Oak Bay.

Oak Bay is bordered by the sea on the east and south, the University of Victoria on the north, and Foul Bay Road on the west. Today it is mostly residential and has become a somewhat exclusive neighbourhood traditionally popular with the influential, the famous and the rich, all of which has created a somewhat stuffy image.

This picture is not totally accurate, for Oak Bay is really neither snobbish nor stuffy. It simply prides itself on its teas, its stately homes, its golf courses and its British colonial heritage.

The homes chosen in this section reflect an eclectic mix of residences, from Tod's haunted house on Heron Street to the grand mansions of Beach Drive and York Place. The stories also include one house with a Butchart connection, another which became a shrine to British Columbia's "last real conservative," and a small cottage once owned by a simple washerwoman.

2564 HERON STREET

THE OLDEST HOUSE IN WESTERN CANADA

The John Tod house on Heron Street in Oak Bay today competes with Helmcken House in the city as the oldest structure still standing west of the Great Lakes.

Without dispute, however, John Tod was one of the five original landowners in Oak Bay when he built the house he called "Oak Bay House" between 1850 and 1851. By then he had retired from his position with the Hudson's Bay Company to live on his over-400 acres of Oak Bay farmland some three miles from the company fort. He had purchased this land for the meagre sum of 109 British pounds, and wrote to a friend that he found it to be "tolerably good, and the situation pleasant and healthy."

The house he built had six rooms, constructed in typical Hudson's Bay Company style of squared logs, which were later sheathed with clapboard. Hand-hewn beams supported the ceilings and hand-forged nails secured the windows. Timber was dovetailed, or pegged and half-lapped at the joints. Two thousand square feet in total, the house had two small attics and passages leading off the rooms which all had low, wide doorways. A fireplace built of fieldstone extended the full height of the living room.

The Tod house was built in three sections. The small, rear kitchen was built first, with the larger section facing the street next, followed by the southwest wing with its bay window, being of more usual frame construction.

Tod had already had an active and colourful career with the company before retiring to Oak Bay. He was born in Scotland in 1790 and moved to Fort McLeod in the Peace River district in 1813. Ten years later, the company put him in charge of Fort Alexandria, south of Quesnel. In 1841, Tod replaced the chief trader at Fort Kamloops, Samuel Black, who had been killed there. Tod was a shrewd and able man who dealt easily with the Indians, one of whom later described him as "the ugliest man at Fort Kamloops."

After he retired from the company, he became one of the first members of the legislative council of the colony of Vancouver Island, and in 1856 was appointed a justice of the peace. When British Columbia joined Confederation in 1871, Tod became a member of the first provincial legislative assembly.

Tod was also something of a mystery. Erratic and temperamental by nature, he was reputed to have had seven wives and fathered ten children. Mary Tod Island was named for one of his daughters, and Bowker Creek in Oak Bay is named for John Bowker who married Mary Tod.

Following Tod's death in 1882, some of his property was divided up among his descendants, but by the late 1880s most of the former Tod estate was owned by Alfred Dixon Fuller. In 1892, Fred Pauline and his family moved into Oak Bay House and it is through this family's collection of memorabilia that the first photographs of the old Tod House came to light. Photographs of the Pauline family on the porch show an older version of the home, for it was not until the 1920s or 1930s that the house became more colonial in style, with further alterations being made over subsequent years.

2564 Heron Street

For many of those years, there were regular reports of strange occurrences at Tod House, and then in 1952 when excavations for a heating oil tank were dug, a skeleton believed to be that of a native Indian woman was discovered. Subsequent owners and tenants of Tod's house have reported many ghostly happenings, including a rocking chair that suddenly began rocking back and forth for no apparent reason, and the latch on the basement door lifting and dropping. One tenant frequently witnessed cups and saucers rattling in the dresser with no obvious cause.

One Christmas morning in the 1940s, the owners found all their cards and tree decorations piled in a heap on the floor. In 1945, two Canadian air force men stayed overnight at the house and were awakened to the sound of rattling chains. They believed they then saw a native Indian woman, with arms outstretched, who seemed to be pleading for help.

Local newspapers have delighted in reporting these happenings with headlines such as "Victoria Ghost House Antics Excite the Interest of Psychic Experts" and "Haunted House Stirred by Strange Events." Every Halloween there is a renewed interest in Oak Bay's most famous haunted house.

As a point of historic interest, a cherry tree growing on the Tod property was reputed to have been planted there by John Tod in 1858.

Since 1975, the Oak Bay municipality and the province of British Columbia have jointly owned this historic building and more restoration work has been carried out on the house which is currently rented.

1932 ST. ANN STREET

AN ARTIST'S TREASURE BOX

Number 1932 St. Ann Street in Oak Bay, built in 1911-12 along with its neighbour, number 1828, by contractors H. Bunting & Son, has a recent new owner with an artistic interest in heritage homes. An awareness of both its architectural and historical importance for the neighbourhood has resulted.

Number 1932 is a variation of the California bungalow style and was built as a speculative investment. Soon after completion, it was purchased by Alfred Carmichael and his wife, Kathleen, after they left Port Alberni and settled in Victoria with their family. During their years in residence, the Carmichaels kept a cow and chickens on their acreage, and their garden was taken care of by a Chinese gardener named Hang Sing.

Alfred Carmichael was an Irishman from Belfast, born in 1874, the son of a flour mill owner. Soon after his father's death, sixteen-year-old Alfred headed for Canada to make his fortune. He arrived in 1890 and contacted a cousin, Herbert Carmichael, who had preceded him. Herbert Carmichael later became the provincial assayer.

After trying various menial jobs in Victoria, Alfred began work at the Aberdeen Salmon Cannery on the Skeena River, and was eventually employed by Robert Woods, the contractor who was building the first paper mill in British Columbia on the Somass River in Port Alberni. Cousin Herbert was the organizer of the mill company but money was tight and the mill lacked the right machinery to make paper from wood pulp so materials such as rags and old rope were being used. Eventually the mill was forced to close down, and Alfred began operating a sawmill close by because logs were cheap.

Alfred was also leading something of an adventurous life during this period helping to survey the area for coastal water-power sites. He later crossed in a small skiff from Texada Island to Powell River to stake out a site for a Victoria syndicate. During the 1890s, he accompanied missionary Melvin Swartout on journeys along the west coast of Vancouver Island and the material they gathered was published in 1922 in a book entitled *Indian Legends of Vancouver Island.*

In 1899, Alfred headed for Atlin where he prospected and mined for the next eight years. In addition, he did some copper prospecting and timber cruising on the Queen Charlotte Islands, and with a partner staked out twenty-two square miles of timber. By 1908 he had earned a contract with the Canadian Pacific Railway to clear the last eight miles of right-of-way for the extension of the Esquimalt and Nanaimo Railway into Port Alberni. His partner by then was a future lieutenant-governor, Colonel Charles A. Moorhead. Back in Port Alberni, he organized the real estate company known as Carmichael and Moorhead Limited and was responsible for clearing the townsite and rough-grading many of the roads.

On April 7, 1909, Alfred married Kathleen Withers, and soon afterward the couple moved to Victoria. During a trip to London, England, in 1911-

1912, Alfred made return reservations aboard the *Titanic* but luckily, because of delays in his business, he was forced to cancel his passage and returned later on the *Cedric.*

From 1914 until 1923, Alfred was the manager of the Franco-Canadian Trust Company in Victoria, as well as the Vancouver Island Fruit Lands Limited and Uplands Limited. Through these latter two land-acquisition and development companies, he and his associates acquired approximately 30,000 acres of land on Vancouver Island which they sold at a profit of $3 an acre to the Franco-Canadian company. Part of their payment was in Uplands shares.

In 1923, the firm of Carmichael and Company Limited was incorporated. In 1926 Alfred formed a partnership with David Leeming, later a mayor of Victoria, 1931 to 1936, in organizing Oak Bay Lands Limited. This company bought 400 Oak Bay tax sale lots for $63,000 in 1926 and Carmichael and Leeming sold off $22,000 worth by auction in just two days from a tent on Oak Bay Avenue. In 1929, however, during the real estate slump, many of these lots lost their value.

Alfred Carmichael, an entrepreneur of note, was also the president of the Victoria Rotary Club in 1929 and president of the Victoria Real Estate Board in 1927, 1931, and 1932. In 1952, because of a heart condition, he was forced to retire from business and his only surviving son, David, took over. Another son had been lost while flying anti-submarine patrols in the Mediterranean during the Second World War, and his daughter was drowned in a yachting accident off Orcas Island in 1952. Kathleen Carmichael died in 1953, and Alfred died at the age of eighty-eight in 1963. He had moved out of his St. Ann house the previous fall.

Much of his property on the south side of the house was then subdivided. In 1985, Don and Patty Wells purchased this heritage home and began some major renovation work. They were only the third owners of the home.

The house came with many delights such as a rhododendron hedge planted by the Carmichaels in 1941. An old magnolia tree, which is on the south side of the house, is reportedly the largest on Vancouver Island, and was added to the Oak Bay heritage register in 1995. An extra feature is the stone wall which now stretches across the two houses in front, and affords privacy to 1932 St. Ann, set high above the road on its rocky promontory. The interior of the house has a pleasant, filled-in porch believed to have been covered in because of the famous "Big Snow" of 1916. There is also an intriguing inglenook with a fireplace flanked by benches and leaded glass-fronted cupboards on both sides. Half walls separate living and dining rooms.

A dormer is utilized as an art studio for the current owner of this charming house, Lynn Gordon-Findlay, the talented illustrator of this book, who refers to her home as "a box of treasures." She is delighted with its warm ambience and especially its fascinating heritage.

1932 St. Ann Street

2031 RUNNYMEDE AVENUE

THE OAK BAY HOUSE WITH A BUTCHART CONNECTION

Number 2031 Runnymede Avenue, known as "Blair Gowie," was built for $10,000 in 1916 for Harry and Jennie Ross. Jennie Ross was a daughter of Robert and Jenny Butchart of Butchart Gardens fame, and the history of this interesting house reflects this floral connection.

The house was designed by Samuel Maclure in Italian Renaissance style with a prominent Palladian window over the large porte cochere. In 1926, Maclure designed some alterations to the original plan, and in 1952 a garage and playroom were added on one side; a carport was built in 1962. The gardens, which have been well maintained throughout the years, remain a typical Butchart treasure.

When Jennie and Harry Ross were in residence, Harry was financial secretary and treasurer of the Vancouver Portland Cement Co. Ltd. at Tod Inlet where his father-in-law was manager. Harry also made money from wise stock investments.

The Rosses' home reflected their opulent lifestyle with many touches such as the elegant Heintzmann piano in the large living room. The breakfast/sitting room overlooked the rock garden and lawn. Their housekeeper lived in accommodation downstairs with a sitting room that also overlooked the delights of the garden. At one time their acreage stretched all the way down to Victoria Avenue.

The Rosses' Chow dog, named "Woo," became quite famous during those years because of an encounter he once had with a cougar roaming in the neighbourhood. Woo came out the winner, completely unscathed. The cougar did not fare quite so well because Woo had very long claws. Following this episode, neighbours feared for the safety of their house cats because after Woo's tangle with the cougar he imagined that all cats of whatever size were his enemies and he wanted to attack them all. Jennie, who was an avid knitter, decided to knit mittens for her dog which he always wore outside to cover his claws.

Jennie and Harry Ross had one son, Ian, who inherited Butchart Gardens from his grandfather on his twenty-first birthday. After returning from wartime service, he set about the phenomenal task of restoring the gardens after years of neglect. Upon Ian Ross' death in the 1990s, son Christopher Ross, a pyrotechnic genius who turned the Butchart fireworks display into a world-famous event, carried on the traditions of excellence at the gardens until his own untimely death in 2000.

Both Jennie Ross and her sister Mary, who had married William Todd in 1910, had inherited the adventurous spirit of their mother, Jenny Butchart. Following Harry Ross' death in the 1930s, Jennie became involved with the handsome and dashing Andre Chirinsky-Chikhmatoff, an impoverished Russian prince. Her choice of partner caused something of a family uproar because she was by then forty-nine and he was only twenty- eight, a scenario that was not acceptable by the standards of the day.

2031 Runnymede Avenue

However, strong-willed Jennie went ahead and married her prince. They had met in Toronto, she a fiery, impulsive woman, and he a Russian gentleman who enjoyed fast-paced living in big cities and the company of beautiful women. Back in quiet Victoria and settled in their Runnymede home, their marriage was doomed but, like so many impoverished members of European royal families, Andre was largely at the mercy of his capricious wife whose money was paying for his elegant lifestyle.

When the prince finally decided to leave for New York and Paris, Jennie stayed at Blair Gowie refusing to accompany him, perhaps realizing her mistake and that the marriage was already over. Eventually they divorced, thus ending a somewhat short-lived but romantic Butchart family connection with royalty. Jennie stayed on in the Runnymede house until just before the Second World War.

Later owners of Blair Gowie were the Fee family, and then the Ellis family who bought the property in 1959 and moved in in 1960. Today, the world-famous Butchart Gardens are still family owned and run, and Jennie (Butchart) Ross' house on Runnymede Avenue in Oak Bay remains a delightful single-family dwelling enjoyed by Mrs. Ellis, who takes great pride in her home and its heritage.

And what of the name Blair Gowie? Harry Ross' family was from Blairgowrie in Scotland situated at the foothills of the Grampians in Perthshire, and that may well have been the reason for the choice of name for the house, even though an "r" was omitted. The origin of Blairgowrie's name is uncertain, but two suggestions have been offered, one being "The Plain of the Goats" and the other "The Battlefield."

Today, neither seems very appropriate to describe this beautiful home on Runnymede Avenue.

2391 BEACH DRIVE

A HOUSE OF SUBSTANCE

The magnificent Samuel Maclure house at 2391 Beach Drive was built in 1914 for Roderick D. Finlayson, the son of the Honourable Roderick Finlayson, former agent and chief factor of the Hudson's Bay Company and one-time mayor of Victoria. Finlayson senior was also the man who, following the death of Chief Factor Charles Ross, had been put in charge of Fort Victoria and, under his able guidance, the fort flourished and eventually became a town.

He and his wife, the former Sarah Work, produced four sons and seven daughters, all of whom were brought up at the Finlayson residence, built in the late 1850s and situated between Government and Douglas Street. At that time, the house was bounded by meadows and orchards. It was there that their son, Roderick Duncan, was born in 1867.

R.D. Finlayson worked for many years with Turner, Beaton & Company, a drygoods firm, but upon the death of his father in 1892, he retired to manage the family estate. Then, in 1914, he hired Samuel Maclure to design a substantial home on Beach Drive in the then-popular Tudor style. In that particular year, Maclure was experiencing a quiet time in his business. The war had brought about a real estate collapse, and his Vancouver partner, Charles Croker Fox, had left for the front lines in France. Maclure, with more time than usual to spare, poured his soul into the Beach Drive home, including many features that he had not brought to his other designs. In 1916, Fox was killed in action, and it then seemed that the Finlayson house became Maclure's memorial to his friend and partner. Unfortunately Finlayson was only able to enjoy his new home for two years and died there in 1916.

The building is visible from both Beach Drive and the Esplanade, and today a separate two-car garage matching the style of the house, even down to the chimney, faces Beach Drive.

The extensive grounds once covered four lots, but in 1986 the property was subdivided and now new homes have been built on the Esplanade side, almost obliterating the Finlayson house from view. On closer inspection, one can still see the handsome porte- cochere, the four substantial chimneys and the heavy roof elements. Well-maintained grounds contribute to the image of Oak Bay at its best.

During the 1930s and 1940s, the house was owned and lived in by members of the Pendray family, whose former family home on Belleville Street was best known as the Captain's Palace restaurant.

As a point of historic interest, an original bronze and art glass light fixture with Quezal shades from the dining room of the Finlayson house is today a part of the history collection at the Royal B.C. Museum. It was acquired by the museum from a neighbour who had owned it and had it rewired, long after the days when it had graced the Finlayson dining room.

In addition to this grand mansion on Beach Drive perpetuating the name of Finlayson, are Finlayson Arm, Mount Finlayson, Finlayson Channel in Milbanke Sound and Finlayson Road in Victoria.

2391 Beach Drive

ANNANDALE

THE PRESTIGIOUS MEN OF YORK PLACE

The house known as "Annandale" on York Place is described by Stuart Stark in his book on Oak Bay heritage homes as being "probably the most historically significant house in Oak Bay."

It was one of a pair of identical homes built in 1897-98 for two very important men, the Honourable Frederick Peters, former premier and attorney-general of Prince Edward Island and Sir Charles Hibbert Tupper, a former minister of justice for the Dominion of Canada and son of Sir Charles Tupper, a Father of Confederation and prime minister of Canada in 1896. Peters named his home "Garrison House" and Tupper called his Annandale.

During the 1930s, Garrison House became a girls' school for a while, but eventually was demolished. Annandale, although converted to suites today, is still owner occupied and stands on its majestic site on York Place.

Shortly after arriving on the west coast in the 1890s, Tupper and Peters became partners in a Victoria law firm. While deciding on a place to live, they stayed for a while with their families at the Mount Baker Hotel and there had conversations with Francis Rattenbury and his partner, John Gerhard Tiarks. This led them to hire Tiarks to design and build their matching homes on land which then extended from York Place through to Prospect Place.

A brief description of the houses stated that each covered a space of over 100 feet by 70 feet at ground level. A flight of steps led to a spacious veranda and the front door which opened into a panelled hall with large fireplace. To the right and left of the hall were the drawing room and dining room, each with large bay windows. The folding doors leading to these rooms could be opened up if required, creating one enormous room of some 50 feet by 20 feet.

There was a cedar-panelled library in each house, and behind the dining room were a sitting room, scullery, larders, kitchen, and storerooms. Tudor arches throughout added charm. The main floor also had five bedrooms and dressing rooms, while on the upper floor were servants' bedrooms, a bathroom, a children's playroom and linen rooms. In winter time, the verandas were often entirely enclosed with "glazed sashes" if necessary, thereby becoming what was described as a comfortable winter promenade.

Surprisingly, these two grand mansions were described simply as bungalows in Rattenbury's album of houses.

From 1911 until 1955, Annandale was owned by the Scott family (the Scott Block at Douglas and Hillside is named for Mr. Scott). When a Scott daughter married into the Crane family, the large property was subdivided but about one-quarter of the original land was left with the house. The Cranes built a new house on the other three-quarters of the land.

The Cranes' former home burned to the ground some time later, but the carriage house which once belonged to Annandale still stands on the old

1587/1595 York Place

Crane property. It was built in Queen Anne style with stained-glass windows and a small balcony and there are living quarters above.

Perhaps one of Annandale's greatest claims to fame, quite apart from its architectural significance in the municipality, is the fact that the original owner's father, Sir Charles Tupper, dined there in the formal dining room on many an occasion. As Canada's sixth prime minister Tupper, who was then seventy-five years old, fought a valiant battle for the Conservatives with his powers of oratory and deep knowledge of political history. He was a man of vision who had always spoken strongly in favour of a trans-continental railway and a future in which Canada would be trading across the Pacific to the Orient. Upon his death in England in 1915, he was acclaimed as "Canada's Grand Old Man." As a baronet of the United Kingdom and an imperial privy councillor, his body was brought back to Canada on the deck of a battleship, a distinct honour for a Canadian who had once held the highest office in the nation – and who had frequently dined at the home of his son on York Place in Oak Bay.

For all of the above reasons, this house is one that should be taken care of and preserved as a piece of important Canadian history.

356 NEWPORT AVENUE

A MEMORIAL TO BC'S LAST REAL TORY

When Herbert Anscomb lived at 356 Newport Avenue from the 1920s until his death in 1972, the Union Jack always flew from the flagpole. He insisted upon flying it rather than the Maple Leaf because his British background and strong conservative views were always paramount in his life.

Anscomb was perhaps one of the most colourful politicians to grace the halls of the Legislative Buildings, and his 27-year political career earned him the title of "one of the last real Conservatives" in B.C. He was by nature a very simple man who deplored extravagance and waste. He always drove an old car and avoided the company of the well-to-do. His one deviation from this path came in death. He had instructed his executors to bury him in an elaborate, $900 solid-walnut coffin which weighed more than 700 pounds. After his memorial service at St. Mary's Church in Oak Bay, this purple-draped coffin was carried to Ross Bay Cemetery where it was placed in a solid granite mausoleum beside his wife who had predeceased him in 1956.

During the Anscomb years, 356 Newport Avenue saw many a political gathering, but the house was also a haven of privacy for Herbert. His home allowed him to escape from what he described once as his disillusionment in politics which were often steeped in hypocrisy. He savoured the privacy his home allowed him. There, he and his beloved wife, "Birdie" (the former A.M. Brooker), whom he married in December of 1925, could forget all about the many social and business events on his calendar.

In public life, he was truly a man who "walked with Kings, yet never lost the common touch" for, among those he had played host to during his term as Victoria's mayor were the Right Honourable Winston Churchill, Sir Arthur Currie, Lord and Lady Willingdon (the governor general and his wife), and the King and Queen of Siam.

Anscomb was born in England in 1892 and was indoctrinated into the political scene as a child, his father being both alderman and mayor of Maidstone. Because his mother died when he was five and his father later suffered a stroke confining him to a wheelchair, young Herbert was raised by an older step-sister.

In 1911 he came to Canada aboard the S.S. *Lake Champlain.* Once in Victoria, he became bookkeeper at the Victoria Phoenix Brewing Company and later articled as a chartered accountant. From 1918 to 1928, he was both accountant and manager of that company. Ironically, many of those years were Prohibition years when liquor was considered to be the "ruination of man." Herbert Anscomb himself never drank.

His political career began in 1925 as reeve of Oak Bay, but his campaign gave him his first taste of dirty politics and smear campaigns. The opposing candidate's followers complained that Anscomb should not be running because he did not actually live in Oak Bay at that time. In addition, they did not want a "brewery man" as their reeve. The electorate ignored these remarks, however, and gave Anscomb a resounding victory and, at age thirty-three, he became the youngest reeve to hold office.

He worked hard for Oak Bay during his term and achieved a number of victories. He was so highly thought of that even the citizens of Victoria were looking to him as a possible candidate for mayor. By then, the Anscombs had moved into their Newport Avenue home. On one occasion, a delegation of forty Victoria citizens presented themselves at the front door of his house with a petition signed by 2,732 Victoria ratepayers, asking him to run for mayor of Victoria. This in itself was a unique occurrence and Anscomb felt extremely honoured. He waited one more year, however, before taking up the challenge, and in November of 1928 was elected mayor of Victoria. He then proceeded to run what he termed his "business council" for the city between 1928 and 1931 and was instrumental in many successful endeavours: he helped establish the new steamship link with the west coast of Vancouver Island and initiated work crews at McDonald Park in James Bay and camps at Waugh Creek and Sooke to ease unemployment problems during the Depression years.

Two of his fondest memories were the consecration ceremony of the new Christ Church Cathedral, and the arrival of the "dial" telephone system; he put through the first dialed call long distance to the lieutenant-governor in Trail, B.C.

On New Year's Day of 1930, Herbert and Birdie Anscomb held a mayor's reception at 356 Newport Avenue from four to six in the afternoon. Well over 500 visitors passed through their doors which was a fine tribute to Anscomb's popularity.

In 1938, Anscomb ran for leadership of the Tory party but was defeated by Pat Maitland and then became the finance critic of the Liberal government. He remained a strong power in opposition until December 1941 when a wartime coalition government of Liberals and Conservatives was formed. Anscomb became one of the three Tory members in the coalition cabinet led by Premier John Hart. After the war the coalition continued and when Pat Maitland died in 1946, it was assumed that Anscomb would take over his position. He was challenged, however, by a certain W.A.C. Bennett, who thought that Anscomb was far too extreme a Conservative to build up the economy of British Columbia.

When Anscomb died in 1972, his estate included many historically valuable and treasured pieces presented to him during his years in public office. There were also several cash bequests and life incomes in his will. Two major Victoria charities benefitted from his generosity: the Canadian National Institute for the Blind in Victoria, and the Queen Alexandra Solarium for Crippled Children.

The Anscombs had had no children, so in his will Anscomb bequeathed his house on Newport Avenue to his friend, Jane Hall, who lived on there until her death in the late 1990s. She maintained the home as a shrine to Anscomb's memory, with photographs and other memorabilia liberally scattered throughout the house. The charming living and dining rooms were separated by glass doors, and both rooms have expansive windows overlooking the golf course, the ocean and the mountains. For many years, Jane enjoyed entertaining her writer friends and sharing with them her memories of Herbert Anscomb, a one-time political giant in British Columbia.

356 Newport Avenue

3150 RUTLAND ROAD

THE PERSONIFICATION OF THE UPLANDS

This elegant home at 3150 Rutland Road was built for Thomas William Paterson after he retired as lieutenant-governor of British Columbia in 1914. The house was designed by architect H.S. Griffith in an adapted mission-revival style with stucco arches forming a large porte cochere and supporting a wrap-around veranda. Its elegant appearance and magnificent garden made the cover of an "Uplands" brochure distributed at the time to promote the area as one of Greater Victoria's most appealing and refined.

Paterson and his wife had previously lived on the north side of the Fort Street hill when that part of the road was still known as Cadboro Bay Road. Their neighbours had included the Creases, the Dunsmuirs and the Harrisons.

Thomas Paterson was born in Scotland in 1851 and came to Canada as a child with his parents. He later went into the contracting business and worked on both the Welland Canal and the Canadian Pacific Railway. In 1893, his was the successful bid for building the Victoria and Sidney Railway. As general manager on that project, he earned both a substantial salary and stock in the company, as well as being contracted to supply all the cordwood fuel for the train engines.

From 1902 to 1907, Paterson served in the British Columbia legislature, representing the Islands as a Liberal, and in 1909 succeeded James Dunsmuir to become B.C.'s ninth lieutenant-governor. Paterson and his wife, who was the daughter of Senator George Riley, were popular hosts at Government House. During his term in office, Paterson had to spend $36,000 to replace the old cedar fence surrounding Government House with a stone wall because of straying cattle. He also initiated the landscaping of the grounds.

On January 12, 1912, the first professional hockey game west of Toronto and the first ever played on artificial ice was held in Victoria. The ice rink was built at Epworth Street and Cadboro Bay Road by lumber magnate, Joseph Patrick, whose two sons, Lester and Frank, helped popularize the sport in the west. The contestants on that auspicious January night were the Victoria Aristocrats and the New Westminster Royals, and the Honourable T.W. Paterson, in his capacity as lieutenant-governor, was called upon to drop the puck. The Aristocrats lost eight to three.

Paterson had fingers in a number of pies. He owned Moresby Island and enjoyed going there to hunt and fish. He also ran a model farm in Delta where he raised Shorthorn cattle. In his spare time, he enjoyed golf and motoring, both of which were gaining in popularity by the turn of the twentieth century.

As a man of considerable means, it was hardly surprising that he and his wife chose to retire to such an elaborate home in the Uplands. The spectacular view of the waterfront with Mount Baker in the distance, merely enhanced the beauty of their home.

In 1944, architect P.L. James did some alterations to the house, but in 1976, a tragic fire broke out causing over $100,000 worth of damage to the

3150 Rutland Road

kitchen, dining room, and stairway. Much renovation and repair helped to restore the structure. Today, however, the T.W. Paterson house looks somewhat different from the original 1914 home.

2087 BYRON STREET

AN INTRIGUING LITTLE HOUSE WITH A "CLEAN" PAST

There are larger, more imposing houses on Byron Street than the one that once belonged to Fanny Eastman, but certainly none more intriguing. There is, for example, number 2090 Byron, the original home of Frederick Gilbert, a master mariner, or its neighbour at number 2086, "Clifton," once owned by a blacksmith, W.T. Hambley. However, the little gem at number 2087, originally the home of Fanny Eastman, listed in the directories as a "washerwoman," stands out from the rest.

The heritage of her small house encompasses many important aspects of Victoria's history, including the days when the rich and famous rode around the city in grand carriages. However, the original cottage part of the Fanny Eastman house is so small and well hidden today that one might overlook it. In 1992 a much larger addition was built to the rear of the house with a breezeway joining the two structures, but the part of the residence built between 1892 and 1893 is still there on Byron Street, and in 1994 was designated heritage by the Municipality of Oak Bay.

Euphemia (Fanny or Fannie) was born in Mexico in 1843, and arrived in Victoria aboard the steamer the *Pacific* in 1862 via California. She married Thomas Eastman, a butcher, and had four children. By the time Fanny's twenty-one-year-old son Samuel built the Byron Street house for her, Fanny was a widow and her three daughters had already married and left home.

Samuel lived with his mother in the small, 515-square-foot, twelve-by-twenty-foot cottage with only three rooms until the late 1890s at which time he married Jessie Knox Winter, daughter of George Winter. George Winter was a well-known coachman, having served two governors (Kennedy and Seymour), as well as Sir Joseph Trutch, B.C.'s first post-Confederation lieutenant-governor. Mr. Winter lived in a small cottage on the grounds of Government House where Jessie was born in 1873.

Later, Winter went into the hack business for himself at the southeast corner of Cook Street and Fairfield Road. He first rented Ross Bay Villa on Fairfield in 1884, and then moved his family into that home in 1892. (Ross Bay Villa is currently the subject of a restoration plan by the Land Conservancy of British Columbia in partnership with the Hallmark Society and the Old Cemeteries Society.) The Winter business prospered and boasted a large staff which kept the carriages in top-notch condition with their lamps always highly polished.

Samuel Eastman, born to Fanny and Thomas in 1871, had gone to work for the Winter Carriages livery business and there had met Jessie. After their marriage on January 3, 1898, they moved to Montreal Street, and Samuel went into business for himself. Like his father- in-law, he also did well and was a familiar sight around Victoria driving the elite to their weddings, theatre parties or funerals, sitting upright on the driver's box displaying his prominent walrus moustache and elegant top hat.

Both George Winter and Samuel Eastman had a narrow escape from death in May 1896 when the Point Ellice Bridge collapsed, killing over fifty people. Both men were driving carriages that day full of passengers going to the Macaulay Point sham battle for the Queen Victoria birthday celebrations. One of the carriages was stationary on one side of the bridge waiting in line to cross, while the other had just passed over and was safely on the other side when the tragedy struck.

By 1916, Samuel Eastman was running a taxi service described as "a noble collection of hacks," and his mother was happily ensconced in her Byron Street cottage in Oak Bay. It was a friendly, middle-class neighbourhood, away from the hectic pace of the city and suited Fanny admirably. It was rumoured that her son may have built the house for her on Byron Street on purpose because it was well away from town – his mother having had a reputation for running afoul of the law while living in the city. But in the far reaches of Oak Bay, she was well away from the temptations of the city and her past life. When the house was built, it was some thirteen years before incorporation, and development was only just beginning in that area which had once formed part of the Pemberton estate.

However, when Fanny Eastman died at her home in July of 1924 at the age of eighty- one, her obituary praised her as a true Victoria pioneer, and she came across as a very respectable woman. Fanny is buried in Ross Bay Cemetery.

One of her three daughters, Mrs. F.L. Monk, had been living with her in the little Byron Road cottage at the time of her death; another daughter lived on Cadboro Bay Road and a third in Chicago. She was also survived by her son Samuel, five grandchildren and seven great-grandchildren. One of Fanny Eastman's granddaughters was Margaret Salt, a secretary to the Social Court Judges for thirty-four years and, in retirement, a well-known member of the Central Saanich Municipality council during the 1960s and early 1970s prior to her death in 1975.

Mrs. Monk stayed on in the little cottage until the mid-1930s and then for the next forty years the house was owned by portrait artist Maude de K. Paget, who shared the home with her sister. Both those ladies were avid gardeners.

Since the 1970s, Bayne Dean has owned the house and has been responsible for the addition to the rear. During the time that renovation work was taking place, part of the cottage had to be raised near where a porch had once been and a strange discovery was made. Numerous green and lavender medicine bottles, some with Jubilee Pharmacy labels, were discovered. These had once belonged to Fanny Eastman and had probably been disposed of by her while sitting on her porch and tossing the bottles over the side. Many of the medicines in those days were alcohol based, perhaps giving some truth to the rumours that Mrs. Eastman was once a lady who enjoyed her liquor.

2087 Byron Street

1255 VICTORIA AVENUE

THE ALEXANDER WALTER ELLIOT HOUSE

Number 1255 Victoria Avenue was built in 1912 for the sum of $4,800 for a lumber merchant, Alexander Walter Elliot, who owned it for the next twelve years. It was designed by architect R.T. Garrow. Described as Edwardian classic, the house served many purposes, both commercial and residential, prior to the First World War. In 1924 the house was sold to Arthur Wootton, whose son was the well-known Victoria judge, Robert A. Wootton. The judge lived in the Victoria Avenue home until he married and moved to McNeill Avenue.

The house, however, remained in the Wootton family and after Arthur and his wife had both died, Robert purchased it from the estate (which had been divided among the other surviving family members), and he and his wife and their two daughters, Anna and Carol, moved back there. When Mrs. Wootton died in 1967, the house was sold and the judge and his two daughters moved to Faithful Street in Fairfield.

The new purchaser of 1255 Victoria Avenue never actually lived there, but did offer to sell half of the vacant lot on the south side to neighbours so that no other house could be built nearby. His offer was refused and the entire lot was then sold to a developer who built on it immediately. The house was next sold to a bank manager who had hoped to retire there, but he was transferred soon after moving to Victoria, and in 1969, number 1255 was acquired by veterinarian Dr. Alan Hoey, who was also an Oak Bay alderman at one time. In May of 1971, the house was purchased by poet Robin Skelton and his wife, Sylvia, who lived in it until their deaths in the late 1990s.

With so many different owners for the first sixty years of its existence, the house underwent a number of renovations and alterations. In 1924, for instance, a fireplace with a brick chimney was installed on the south wall of the living room. Until then the only fireplaces were in the hall and in an upstairs study, both sharing one granite chimney on the north side.

During the ownership of the bank manager and Dr. Hoey, the kitchen, scullery and butler's pantry were remodelled so that a laundry room opened off the new, much larger, kitchen area. The Skeltons had an electric furnace installed for the hot-water central-heating system, and had the small upper porch glazed to fit the style of the rest of the house. These many alterations did not detract from the distinctive elements of the building where Greek and Roman features are used to great effect. Doric columns still encircle the porch and the soffits are supported by modillion brackets.

During the approximately twenty-five years of Skelton ownership, their home was the gathering place of writers, poets and artists, for Robin and his wife were members of the Limners, a unique group of seventeen artists who worked in eleven different media. The Limners take their name from the travelling journeyman painters of the Middle Ages who earned a living by painting portraits and signs for inns. The Victoria Limners included such esteemed

1255 Victoria Avenue

artists as Pat Martin Bates, Myfanwy Pavelic, Carole Sabiston, and of course Robin and Sylvia Skelton. Their gatherings, often held at the Skeltons' house, were lively and full of enlightening conversation about their varied art forms and latest creations. The home was replete with contemporary Canadian, British, and African art. Sylvia Skelton was a talented calligrapher, and all three Skelton offspring were involved in the arts.

Robin Skelton was born in 1925 in East Yorkshire, England, and attended the University of Leeds and later taught at the University of Manchester. In 1963 he emigrated to Canada and taught for many years at the University of Victoria where he became mentor to many-up-and-coming writers and poets who all held him in high esteem. He was the co-founder of the *Malahat Review* and author of more than 100 published works of poetry, fiction, non-fiction, art criticism and biography. He was well-known for his devotion to the occult and, as a devout follower of Wicca, was a self-confessed, initiated witch. He died on August 22, 1997, at the age of seventy-one.

The Victoria Avenue house was sold following Sylvia Skelton's death a short time after her husband's. The current owner is renovating and restoring this attractive house which has had so many owners throughout its existence. All have undoubtedly left their mark, but none more than the dynamic Skeltons who lived there the longest.

The Final Word

At the end of this fascinating journey into the past of so many residences, I am more than ever convinced that heritage homes and their tales help us to better understand the history of Victoria. In addition, they reveal a great deal about the way we once lived in British Columbia's capital city.

I am also left with the realization that there are many more tales waiting to be told. The fifty houses chosen for this volume merely scratch the surface of Greater Victoria's residential heritage. Since completing the book, I have been approached by numerous owners and other interested parties who would like to have had their house of choice included. Obviously this topic is far from exhausted!

I am pleased that as well as the owners of these homes, there are also a great many organizations in the city and in the municipalities of Saanich, Esquimalt and Oak Bay, who are dedicated to preserving the histories of heritage houses. The Saanich Heritage Foundation, for instance, is one of many such groups which promote the preservation, maintenance and restoration of buildings, structures and land that have been heritage designated, and provide grants to owners of heritage buildings to assist in exterior restoration work. This same dedication and promotion of public awareness and interest in heritage conservation is present in other similar organizations and committees throughout Greater Victoria. It is heartwarming to know so many concerned people wish to ensure that our historic treasures from the past remain for future generations to enjoy.

Under the stewardship of caring owners, these particular "Houses from the Past" (which are a mere sample of what Greater Victoria has to offer) will continue to live, breathe and evolve throughout time.

Bibliography

Barr, Jennifer Nell. *Saanich Heritage Structures: An Inventory,* Victoria, The Corporation of the District of Saanich, 1991.

Barron, Elwyn A., ed. *Deeds of Heroism & Bravery - The Book of Heroes and Personal Daring,* New York and London, Harper Brothers Publishers, 1924.

Castle, Geoffrey, and King, Barry. *Victoria Landmarks,* Victoria, B.C., published by Geoffrey Castle & Barry King, 1985.

Castle, Geoffrey, and King, Barry. *More Victoria Landmarks,* Victoria, B.C., Sono Nis Press, 1988.

City of Victoria Heritage Advisory Committee. *This Old House: An Inventory of Residential Heritage, City of Victoria,* Victoria, B.C., 1979.

Green, Valerie. *No Ordinary People: Victoria's Mayors since 1862,* Victoria, B.C., Beach Holme Publishers, 1992.

Green, Valerie. *The Vantreights: A Daffodil Dynasty,* Victoria, B.C., GAV Publishers, 1997.

Gregson, Harry. *A History of Victoria (1842-1970),* Victoria, B.C., The Victoria Observer Publishing Co. Ltd., 1970.

Hutchison, Bruce. *A Life in the Country,* Vancouver/Toronto, Douglas & McIntyre, 1988.

Jupp, Ursula. *From Cordwood to Campus in Gordon Head, 1852-1959,* Victoria, B.C., published by Ursula Jupp, 1975.

Kluckner, Michael. *Vancouver: The Way it Was,* Vancouver, B.C., Whitecap Books, 1993.

Minaker, Dennis. *The Gorge of Summers Gone - A History of Victoria's Inland Waterway,* Victoria, B.C., Desktop Publishing, 1998.

Segger, Martin. *The Buildings of Samuel Maclure,* Victoria, B.C., Sono Nis Press, 1986.

Segger, Martin & Franklin, Douglas. *Exploring Victoria's Architecture,* Victoria, B.C., Sono Nis Press, 1996.

Stark, Stuart. *Oak Bay's Heritage Buildings; More than just Bricks and Boards,* Victoria, B.C., Hallmark Society, 1994.

Teague, Jarrett Thomas. *Blessings in Plenty - A Life and Park History,* Victoria, B.C., 1998.

ndex